RENEWING PASTORAL PRACTICE

This is the first comprehensive treatment of the relationship between the doctrine of the Trinity and pastoral care and counselling. Neil Pembroke contends that an in-depth reflection on the relational dynamics in the Godhead has the capacity to radically renew pastoral practice.

Pembroke applies the notion of relational space to care in a parish setting. The life of the triune God is defined by both closeness and open space. The divine persons indwell each other in love, but they also provide space for the expression of particularity. This principle of closeness-with-space is applied in three different pastoral contexts, namely, community life, spiritual friendship, and pastoral conversations. The specialized ministry of pastoral counselling is the focus in the second half of the book. Informing the various explorations is the principle of participation through love: the divine persons participate in each other's existence through loving self-communication. Pembroke shows how this trinitarian virtue is at the centre of three key counselling dynamics: the counselling alliance, empathy, and mirroring.

Explorations in Practical, Pastoral and Empirical Theology

Series Editors: Leslie J. Francis, University of Wales, Bangor, UK
and Jeff Astley, University of Durham and Director of the
North of England Institute for Christian Education, UK

Theological reflection on the church's practice is now recognized as a significant element in theological studies in the academy and seminary. Ashgate's new series in practical, pastoral and empirical theology seeks to foster this resurgence of interest and encourage new developments in practical and applied aspects of theology worldwide. This timely series draws together a wide range of disciplinary approaches and empirical studies to embrace contemporary developments including: the expansion of research in empirical theology, psychological theology, ministry studies, public theology, Christian education and faith development; key issues of contemporary society such as health, ethics and the environment; and more traditional areas of concern such as pastoral care and counselling.

Other titles recently published in this series:

Evangelicals Etcetera
Conflict and Conviction in the Church of England's Parties
Kelvin Randall

A Reader on Preaching
Making Connections
Edited by David Day, Jeff Astley and Leslie J. Francis

Engaging with Contemporary Culture
Christianity, Theology and the Concrete Church
Martyn Percy

Congregational Studies in the UK
Christianity in a Post-Christian Context
Edited by Mathew Guest, Karin Tusting and Linda Woodhead

Renewing Pastoral Practice
Trinitarian Perspectives on Pastoral Care and Counselling

NEIL PEMBROKE

ASHGATE

Published by
Ashgate Publishing Limited
Gower House, Croft Road
Aldershot, Hants
GU11 3HR
England

Ashgate Publishing Company
Suite 420
101 Cherry Street
Burlington, VT 05401-4405
USA

Ashgate website: http://www.ashgate.com

British Library Cataloguing in Publication Data
Pembroke, Neil
 Renewing pastoral practice : Trinitarian perspectives on pastoral care and
 counselling. – (Explorations in practical, pastoral and empirical theology)
 1.Pastoral care 2.Pastoral counseling 3.Trinity
 I.Title
 253.5

Library of Congress Cataloging-in-Publication Data
Pembroke, Neil.
 Renewing pastoral practice : Trinitarian perspectives on pastoral care and
counselling / Neil Pembroke.—1st ed.
  p. cm. — (Explorations in practical, pastoral, and empirical theology)
  Includes bibliographical references and index.
  ISBN 0-7546-5565-2 (hardcover : alk. paper)
 1. Pastoral theology. 2. Pastoral counseling. 3. Trinity. I. Title. II. Series.

 BV4011.3.P46 2006
 253—dc22

2005026469

ISBN-13: 978-0-7546-5565-7
ISBN-10: 0-7546-5565-2

Typeset by GCS, Leighton Buzzard, Bedfordshire.
Printed and bound in Great Britain by MPG Books Ltd, Bodmin, Cornwall.

For my whole family, in deep appreciation of each one's love

Contents

Introduction

I have long been convinced of the importance of sustained, in-depth theological reflection on pastoral practice. There is, of course, a variety of options available for such reflection. Some have located theological ethics at the centre of their work.[1] Others have shown how the theology in key biblical narratives can be used in constructing a pastoral theory.[2] Still others have pointed up the importance of political theology.[3]

Here I look to a central doctrine of the Christian faith for guidance in shaping our pastoral theory and practice. I have to say that my interest in the present topic is relatively new. If you had said to me five years ago that I would be writing a book on the Trinity and pastoral care I would have laughed at you. Assuming that you once took a course on the doctrine of the Trinity, it may well be that your experience was somewhat similar to mine. As the professor recounted the attempts throughout the ages to explain how threeness and oneness go together you wondered what in heaven's name any of this had to do with life in the real world. Since in my days as a theological student I failed to get excited about the possibilities of trinitarian theology, for a very long time the thought of picking up a book on this great mystery of our faith never crossed my mind. Everything changed a few years ago, however, when in a postgraduate seminar a colleague of mine used Pat Fox's book *God as Communion* to develop a theology of pastoral leadership.[4] Feeling inspired by the pastoral possibilities, I began to do some research and in the process discovered that there has been a significant turn to the practical by theologians as they develop their trinitarian thinking. This is not some esoteric doctrine, they say, but rather one that is able to richly illuminate and shape contemporary Christian living. In my reading I found a number of interesting applications. Some theologians have addressed such areas as therapy, psychological development and politics.[5] Others have used the doctrine of the Trinity to develop an understanding of ministry and of the various pastoral issues that are involved.[6] Still others have used the light of trinitarian thinking to illumine our general approach to the moral life in both its personal and its socio-political dimensions.[7]

Though these new developments take on a variety of shapes and colours, what unites them is a common concern with relationality. At the heart of the mystery of the triune God is the fact that the Three indwell each other in love and reach out to humankind, calling us to share in their loving communion. Given that relationship is absolutely central in pastoral care, it might be expected that an exploration of the Trinity would be fruitful in this area as well. Identifying what some of these fruits might be is the challenge that is taken up here.

The aim is not simply to point out that the doctrine of the Trinity has relevance for pastoral care and counselling. Rather, I attempt to show how thinking about the Trinity has the capacity to renew our vision of the ministry of care. Taking a trinitarian perspective on this ministry, I suggest, produces insights concerning theory and practice that are simply missed out on by the other approaches we are accustomed to.

In the first part of the book, attention is given to the general ministry of care. Here I shall explore the fundamental issue of *relational space*. In the life of the triune God we find both closeness and open space. The divine persons indwell each other in love, but if there were no space between them their distinctiveness would be lost. The Three draw close to each other through absolute self-giving, and an essential part of this giving to the other is the provision of space in which he or she can express his or her particularity. Here we have the model for human interrelatedness. The principle of closeness-with-space is applied in three different pastoral contexts: community life, spiritual friendship and pastoral conversations.

Within the overarching theme of relational space, a number of important subthemes are developed. The explorations in Chapter 2 will lead us to the notion that pastoral care is polyphonic in nature. *Polyphony* is a musical term that denotes the simultaneous singing or playing of two or more melodic lines of equal importance in the overall structure. In relation to the Trinity, it refers to the way in which simultaneous difference exists in a homogeneous unity. It will be suggested that polyphony is an imprint of the triune God in the ministry of care. That is, faithful and effective pastoral relationships constitute a reflection or a paralleling of the polyphonic relationality in the Godhead. The polyphonic dynamics I shall concentrate on are, first, *wisdom* and *folly* and, secondly, *communion, nearness* and *distance*.

The notion of hospitality will form the focus of Chapter 3. Hospitality requires a spirit of openness to the other. The guest feels at home when she is provided with a creative emptiness. Such emptiness allows her space to be. At the same time, openness has its limits. It is not possible to host destructive attitudes and behaviours. The principle of 'bounded openness' will be applied to the pastoral ministry.

In Chapter 4, the idea of openness to others is developed further. Here, however, our focus will be shifted from pastoral relationships to community in the congregation. The trinitarian dynamics of *kenosis* (self-emptying) and *perichoresis* (mutual indwelling) will be used to inform our understanding of what is required to build Christian community.

In the second part of the book, we will turn our attention to the specialized ministry of pastoral counselling. The principle that will shape our reflections is *participation through love*. The divine persons participate in each other's existence through loving self-communication. This dynamic is also central in a counselling ministry.

The important issue of the counselling alliance will be addressed in Chapter 5. The practice of establishing a 'three-dimensional' alliance consisting of the counsellor, the counsellee and the support person(s) will be explored. These three agents participate through love in the project of healing and growth for the counsellee. This alliance, it will be suggested, mirrors the life of the triune God.

The focus in Chapter 6 is on empathy. The loving participation in the Trinity points to a vitally important function of empathy, namely the overcoming of the experience of isolation and aloneness. An empathic connection with another says, 'You are not alone; I am with you in this.' The trinitarian experience of identity-through-relations will lead us into reflection on another key function of empathy. That key role is the knitting together of the various fragments of the self into a coherent sense of 'I'. Empathy involves more than simply reflecting back elements in a person's sense of identity. It also plays a significant role in forming that identity.

Empathy is central in the therapeutic practice of 'mirroring', to use Heinz Kohut's term. Mirroring involves approval, affirmation and admiration. As Donald Capps has so clearly shown, it is a central pastoral action.[8] In Chapter 7, the thesis will be argued that mirroring is a loving act expressed in the distinct forms of *agape, eros* and *philia*. Divine love also has three forms. The divine persons each share fully in the grace-filled acts of creation, salvation and sanctification. At the same time, they express their love through these actions according to their particularity. 'God is originatively Love as Father, expressively Love as Son, communicatively Love as Spirit: three subjects in the one conscious infinite act of Being-in-love.'[9] The suggestion, then, is that pastoral mirroring provides a reflection of God's love.

These reflections on the theory and practice of pastoral care and counselling are framed by a consideration of two central theological questions, namely, relationality in God and God's participation in human suffering. The scene will be set through a survey of recent attempts by theologians to describe the relational dynamic that is the Trinity. Given that pastoral care, understood in a broad sense, involves the attempt to alleviate human suffering, it seems appropriate to conclude with an analysis of suffering that is guided by trinitarian theology.

The theme of relationality first emerged in the trinitarian reflections of the Cappadocians. It is also at the very centre of the work of contemporary leading lights such as Jürgen Moltmann, Catherine Mowry LaCugna, Ted Peters and David Cunningham (although he prefers the term *participation*). We will begin our explorations by mapping this crucial development in the interpretation of the life of the Trinity.

The following chapters are based on material by the author previously published elsewhere: Chapter 2, on 'Trinity, Polyphony and Pastoral Relationships', *Journal of Pastoral Care and Counseling* 58:4 (2004), pp. 351–61; Chapter 5, on 'A Trinitarian Perspective on the Counseling Alliance in Narrative Therapy', *Journal of Psychology and Christianity* 24:1 (2005), pp. 13–20; and Chapter 7, on 'Trinity, Love and Pastoral Mirroring', *Pastoral Psychology* 53:2 (2004), pp. 163–73.

Notes

1   See D. Browning, *The Moral Context of Care* (Philadelphia: Westminster Press, 1976); idem, *Religious Ethics and Pastoral Care* (Minneapolis: Fortress Press, 1983).

2   See D. Capps, *Life Cycle Theory and Pastoral Care* (Philadelphia: Fortress Press, 1983); idem, *Reframing: A New Method in Pastoral Care* (Minneapolis: Fortress Press, 1990); idem, *The Depleted Self: Sin in a Narcissistic Age* (Minneapolis: Fortress Press, 1993).

3   See L. Graham, *Care of Persons, Care of Worlds* (Nashville, Tenn.: Abingdon Press, 1992); S. Pattison, *Pastoral Care and Liberation Theology* (Cambridge University Press, 1994); J. Poling, *Deliver Us from Evil: Resisting Racial and Gender Oppression* (Minneapolis: Fortress Press, 1996).

4   P. Fox, *God as Communion* (Collegeville, Minn.: Liturgical Press, 2001).

5   See A. Kelly, *The Trinity of Love: A Theology of the Christian God* (Wilmington, Del.: Michael Glazier, 1989).

6   See T. Drilling, *Trinity and Ministry* (Minneapolis: Fortress Press, 1991); P. Fiddes, *Participating in God: A Pastoral Doctrine of the Trinity* (London: Darton, Longman and Todd, 2000).

7   On the personal dimension, see C.M. LaCugna, *God for Us: The Trinity and Christian Life* (HarperSanFrancisco, 1991); D. Cunningham, *These Three Are One: The Practice of Trinitarian Theology* (Oxford: Blackwell, 1998); and C. Gunton, *Intellect and Action* (Edinburgh: T. & T. Clark, 2000), Ch. 6, 'The Church as a School of Virtue? Human Formation in Trinitarian Framework'. On the socio-political dimension, see L. Boff, *Holy Trinity, Perfect Community* (New York: Orbis Books, 2000).

8   See Capps, *The Depleted Self*.

9   Kelly, *The Trinity of Love*, p. 182.

SETTING THE SCENE

Chapter 1

The Renewal of the Doctrine of the Trinity
Relationality and Triune 'Marks'

When I first contemplated turning to trinitarian thinking as a source for pastoral theology, I had in mind a comment by a former colleague of mine, a systematic theologian, that the Trinity is 'all about relationality'. Since the relational element is at the very centre of pastoral work, it seemed to me that the doctrine of the Trinity must have the potential to make a major contribution to pastoral theory and practice. As I began to read up on contemporary trinitarian perspectives, I discovered that most theologians today are convinced that the doctrine of the Trinity is a practical matter. They contend that it is a rich storehouse of insights into the nature of the Christian life. Such a contention will be met with immediate scepticism on the part of many. The Church's teaching on the Trinity, say the sceptics, is the result of the ponderous ruminations of 'some intellectually constipated Greeks and Latins in a bygone era to meet challenges that have long since disappeared'.[1] It is true that the language of the early trinitarian debates was drawn from a metaphysics of substance; such words as *homoousios* and *hypostasis* were at the centre of the theological arguments. But we have moved on from there. *Relationship* has replaced *substance* as the central term. 'Trinitarian theology could be described as par excellence a theology of relationship, which explores mysteries of love, relationship, personhood and communion within the framework of God's self-revelation in the person of Christ and the activity of the Spirit.'[2]

A focus on relationality – both within the Godhead and in God's saving encounter with the world – is the most common way in which theologians seek to renew the doctrine of the Trinity. Some theologians, however, while fully acknowledging the value in such an approach, also turn to the old method of the *vestigia trinitatis* (Augustine) as a way of breathing new life into trinitarian theology.[3] The argument here is that we can find parallels in human life to the central dynamics in the life of the Godhead. In reflecting on the interpersonal life of human beings – especially in its familial and communal dimensions – it is possible to identify the 'marks' of the Trinity. As my thinking on the relationship between the doctrine of the Trinity and pastoral praxis began to take shape, this idea of paralleling became increasingly important. I began to see that positive relational dynamics in pastoral encounters can be viewed as mirroring the inner life of God.

I am not pretending to present here anything like a full treatment of the renewal of the doctrine of the Trinity. That story is a complicated one; it is a tale with many a twist and turn, and it features a very large number of characters. My aim is simply to sketch the outlines of this story through concentrating on two issues that are central in the pastoral theology that I practise in the rest of this book.

In order to get ourselves situated in the plot that is the renewal of trinitarian theology, it is necessary to attend to two images of God that have played leading roles, namely God as supreme substance and God as absolute subject.[4] Both these images are nuclei around which important conceptions of the triune God have been formed. But neither conception has the capacity to support a social understanding of the Trinity. We understand a great deal about the development of trinitarian theology when we appreciate the role that the notions of substance, subject and communion have played in it.

God as Supreme Substance

The notion of God as the supreme substance in the world, Jürgen Moltmann observes, is grounded in Greek philosophy and religion.[5] The Greeks thought of the world as a cosmos that has an essential order established on the basis of eternal laws. At the centre of life in the cosmos are the gods, with whom human beings live in fellowship to the extent that they express in the way that they live the order and movements of the cosmos. The divine nature that is present in all worldly movements is 'one, necessary, immovable, infinite, unconditional, immortal and impassible'.[6] This supreme substance is at the centre of the cosmos.

From very early in the history of Christian thought the category of substance featured in trinitarian formulations. Tertullian (c.160–c.220) sought to capture the essence of the Trinity with the formula *una substantia, tres personae*. The one indivisible, homogeneous divine substance exists as three individual persons. The early Christological controversies that sparked the first sustained theological reflection on the nature of the Trinity were also grounded in a substantialist understanding of God. A central figure in these debates was the distinguished theologian from Alexandria in Egypt, Arius (c.270–336). According to Arius, though Jesus was God in that he shared the divine nature, he was in fact a created God. 'There is ... a gulf at the most fundamental level of being between the Father and the Son.'[7] The incarnation in Jesus of Nazareth was the incarnation of the Logos, but not that of God the Creator. The Logos is created *ex nihilo*, and hence Arius can say that 'there was a time when the Logos was not'. 'The Logos or Son participates in the grace, but not the essence of the Father.'[8] For Arius, then, Christ was God only 'in an honorary way', in the words of Paul Fiddes.

At the Council of Nicea in 325 it was affirmed that the Son is *homoousios* (of one substance) with the Father. The Bishop of Alexandria, Athanasius (295–373), became the champion of the Nicean doctrine. His refutation of Arianism centred on the issue of salvation.[9] If the Word is only a created being, no matter how exalted, our salvation is placed under threat. Only if the Logos is fully divine can he bring to the world a true revelation of God. Similarly, the re-creation of human nature in the image of God requires a fully divine mediator, and the victory over death requires the death and resurrection of the Lord of life himself. The trinitarian formula that Athanasius developed to support his theology of salvation is as follows. The one divine *ousia* (substance), infinite, simple and indivisible, is at once Father, Son and

Holy Spirit. That is, Father, Son and Holy Spirit together form a consubstantial triad. All three are distinct, and yet all three share in the one divine essence.

Though this formula affirms that both the Son and the Spirit are, along with the Father, fully divine, it does not tell us *how* the three persons constitute the one God.[10] Here the Cappadocians, Basil the Great (d. 379), his brother Gregory of Nyssa (d. 394) and Gregory of Nazianzus (d. 390), stepped in and carried the doctrine further along. Following Athanasius, the Cappadocians affirmed that not only is the Son consubstantial with the Father, but the Spirit also. Against this, the Arians had argued that if the Holy Spirit shared the same substance as the Father then this could only be because the Spirit was generated. But if the Spirit is generated he is a Son, and the Father has two Sons. What the Cappadocians came up with is that the Son is generated, but the Spirit 'proceeds' from the Father. The formula that they developed represents a middle path between tritheism on the one side and Sabellianism (the three persons are merely different modes of the revelation of the one God) on the other.[11] According to the Cappadocians, the triune God is one *ousia* but three *hypostases* (realities). The genius in this formulation is that it maintains both the unity of God and the full and complete being of each of the persons. The Trinity, according to the Cappadocians, consists of 'persons in communion' (*hypostases en koinonia*). Through the use of *hypostasis* they ensured that each person was granted full being. The unity in the triune God was protected through the employment of *koinonia*.

Through a new approach to personhood in the Trinity, the Cappadocian theologians were able to develop a relational understanding of God. Whereas the theologians in the West located the ontological principle of God in the substance of God (*una substantia, tres personae*), they turned to the *hypostasis*. That is to say, the Cappadocians related the ontological dimension in God to the personhood in God. It is God as Father, not as substance, who begets the Son and breathes out the Spirit.

God as Absolute Subject

The notion of God as substance was grounded in a view of the world as cosmos. God is placed at the centre of an ordered universe. With the rise of the scientific method, however, human persons begin to see themselves as at the centre of the world. As they gain more and more knowledge of how it works, they have the means of exerting a higher level of control over it. In this way, they begin to see it as *their* world. 'The centre of this world and its point of reference', Moltmann notes, 'is the human subject, not a supreme substance.'[12]

In this situation in which the human experiences herself as subject over against a world of objects, it is natural that those who believe in God would see the divine as an archetype of themselves. God is the infinite, perfect and absolute subject. In the older metaphysics, God is the ground of the world, the centre point of an ordered universe. Now the divine is construed as the ground of the soul.[13] In the new paradigm, the human person comes to herself, expresses her inherent dignity, through the exercise of reason and free will. Moltmann puts it well: 'God, thought of as subject, with perfect reason and free will, is in actual fact the archetype of the free, reasonable, sovereign person, who has complete disposal over himself.'[14]

This notion of God as absolute subject undergirds Karl Rahner's attempt at renewal of the doctrine of the Trinity.[15] The story of the Trinity, for Rahner, is the story of God's self-communication to humanity. This is not only a communication of the divine nature, but moreover a person-to-person communication. God's gift of Godself is understood as a 'free personal act' and therefore as a 'communication of "persons"'.[16] What God offers to us is not simply some share of Godself; rather, this is truly a *self*-communication. In a word, God bestows the Godself. Out of love for humanity God freely gives of Godself for our salvation. 'It is a self-communication in which the God who manifests himself "is there" as self-uttered truth and as freely, historically disposing sovereignty.'[17] The divine self-communication to human persons, Rahner points out, carries within itself true distinctions. This is what the biblical testimony to Father, Son, and Holy Spirit means. God gives Godself to us through the Word and in the power of the Holy Spirit. There is, then, 'a double mediation' within this self-communication.[18]

What we have here is the emergence of a relational paradigm for trinitarian theology. The shortcoming in Rahner's approach, however, is that he is not able to include fully the communion of the three Persons in his system. 'It is inescapably obvious', comments Jürgen Moltmann, 'that, for the sake of the identity of the self-communicating divine subject, Rahner has to surrender the interpersonal communion of the triune God.'[19] Moltmann makes the point – and this for me is the heart of the matter – that what needs to be placed firmly at the centre of any attempt to renew the doctrine of the Trinity is the notion that the ground of divine life is to be found in the eternal *perichoresis* of the Father, the Son and the Holy Spirit. The mutual indwelling of the Three binds them together in fellowship or communion of a unique or special kind. Not only should we seek to emulate this communion in our human relationships; we are drawn into it through the power of the Holy Spirit. The fellowship of the triune God is an open one:

> The fellowship of the triune God is so open and inviting that it is depicted in the fellowship of the Holy Spirit which human beings experience with one another – 'as you, Father, are in me and I in you' – and takes this true human fellowship into itself and gives it a share in itself: 'that they may also be *in us*'.[20]

Relationality is the central term in the new approach to the doctrine of the Trinity. The older metaphysic of substance, despite its usefulness in the task of asserting the equality of the Three, is spoilt by the image of God that is associated with it. God as substance speaks of an isolated, passionless monad. The modern European metaphysic of subjectivity allows for the idea of a person to person communication, but ultimately it leads away from the interpersonal relations of the triune God. It is the notion of fellowship or communion that is primary in the renewal of trinitarian thinking.

God as Open Communion

Catherine Mowry LaCugna, a central figure in the renewal of the doctrine of the Trinity, builds her relational theology of God around the notion of persons in communion. LaCugna defines what she means by personhood over against Aquinas and others who construe person as an individual who is self-possessed in self-knowledge and self-love.[21] She argues that a concept of person adequate for the task of describing the communion of divine and human persons must incorporate the notions of intersubjectivity, ecstasis and catholicity.[22] Persons, she notes first, are not isolated, self-contained entities. To be a person is to be in relationship. Here LaCugna picks up on an idea that was first developed by dialogical philosophers such as Buber, Rosenzweig and Macmurray. They asserted that prior to the ego and subjectivity is the I–Thou relation. Ted Peters captures well this dialogical understanding of the human person when he observes: 'Our identity grows continually through interaction with other individuals ... Gone is the image of the self-defined and autonomous individual, the island of personhood standing over against society.'[23]

Ecstasis refers to the human capacity for self-transcendence. To be a person is to reach beyond oneself, to go out to others in love. 'To exist as a person is to be referred to others; the negation and dissolution of personhood is total self-reference.'[24] Catholicity, finally, has two aspects. First, the true nature of a person is expressed in her desire to be inclusive of everything in the world. Secondly, 'the inclusive, catholic person expresses the totality of a nature; each human person exemplifies what it means to be human'.[25]

Persons exist for communion. Human life expresses its true nature and meaning when persons come together in a fellowship of love. The essential meaning of the Trinity for LaCugna is that God reaches out to the world in Christ and through the power and presence of the Spirit calling all creatures into a loving communion of human and divine persons.

> The perfection of God is the perfection of love, of communion, of personhood. Divine perfection is the antithesis of self-sufficiency, rather it is the absolute capacity to be who and what one is by being for and from another. The living God is the God who is alive in relationship, alive in communion with the creature, alive with desire for union with every creature.[26]

God is love and it is therefore the nature of God to communicate Godself to every living creature. LaCugna sees Rahner's emphasis on God's self-communication as the key to revitalizing the doctrine of the Trinity.[27] She contends, however, that we need to go beyond Rahner in one important aspect. This has to do with the way in which he establishes the relationship between the immanent Trinity and the economic Trinity. The former term refers to the inner life of God – God *in se*; the latter indicates God's saving work in the world, incorporating creation, redemption, and consummation – God *ad extra*. Rahner wants to take us beyond a God locked up inside itself through his principle that 'the "economic" Trinity is the "immanent" Trinity and the "immanent" Trinity is the "economic" Trinity'.[28] The mystery of God's grace and that of God in Godself are one and the same mystery. What we encounter in God's self-communication is not a copy of the inner Trinity, but this Trinity itself.

This is well and good as far as it goes, says LaCugna, but she is dissatisfied with the fact that Rahner still seems to hold on to two levels within the one self-communication of God in the economy of Christ and the Spirit.[29] There is God's self-communication *in se*, and there is God's self-communication *ad extra* (the missions of Word and Spirit). If we are to push forward in developing the practical and relational potential in the doctrine of the Trinity, LaCugna argues, we need to drop the terms economic Trinity and immanent Trinity altogether. In the end, she says, 'to speak about God in immanent trinitarian terms is nothing more than to speak about God's life with us in the economy of Christ and the Spirit'.[30]

LaCugna's preference is to take up in a revised form the old terms of *oikonomia* and *theologia*. Her premise is that there is no need to reflect on the inner life of God; the mystery of God (*theologia*) is simply what we know of God through God's self-communication in Christ and the Spirit.

> *Oikonomia* is not the Trinity *ad extra* but the comprehensive plan of God reaching from creation to consummation, in which God and all creatures are destined to exist together in the mystery of love and communion. Similarly, *theologia* is not the Trinity *in se*, but, much more modestly and simply, the mystery of God. As we know from the experience of being redeemed by God through Jesus Christ, the mystery of God is the mystery of God with us.[31]

For a number of theologians, this is going too far. The immanent Trinity cannot simply be collapsed into the economic Trinity. They would want to assert quite strongly – and I believe they are right in this – that there is a communal God apart from the God who calls us into communion.[32] There are two major reasons why it is important to make this point. First, the notion of an immanent Trinity protects divine freedom; and, secondly, it allows the world to be itself. A sovereign God freely chooses to communicate the Godself to the world. If all we have is an economic Trinity, however, God becomes dependent on God's historical manifestation. That is, God *must* have the divine mission to the world to be God. The being of God gets absorbed into the event of revelation; God *in se* disappears and we are left only with God's gracious communication with the world. 'If ... our knowledge of God is limited to the economy, there is then no ontic background to the historical revelation and no knowledge of an ontological nature of God in himself; in fact no such God exists.'[33]

As well as this concern to protect the freedom of God, there is also a need to safeguard the integrity of the world.[34] When there is a 'space' between God and the world, God can be Godself and the world itself. Maintaining the notion of an immanent Trinity ensures the relative independence and integrity of worldly reality. 'It is because God is a communion of love prior to and in independence of the creation', writes Colin Gunton, 'that God can enable the creation to be itself.'[35]

The line that I pursue is as follows. The notion of the immanent Trinity is maintained, but not as a divine life locked up inside itself. God reaches out in love to the world through Christ and the Spirit and invites us to share in the communion of God's love. David Cunningham captures this notion of an interlocking connection between the inner life of God and God for us through the metaphor of 'producing'.[36] He observes that the divine 'production' encompasses both 'God producing God' and 'God producing the world'. The idea of the production of the world points not only to the act of creation, but also to the missions of the Word and the Spirit.

'God producing God' is Cunningham's way of referring to Aquinas's understanding of the processions and relations within God. In Aquinas's scheme, God produces God through the processions of 'begetting' (the Word) and 'breathing forth' (the Spirit).[37] These processions imply, in turn, four kinds of 'real relation', namely begetting, being begotten, breathing out and being breathed. There are, however, only three unique relations because the actions through which the Word and the Spirit are produced (begetting and breathing out respectively) are of the same general type. Thus the three unique relations are begetting (which includes breathing out), being begotten and being breathed forth. What Aquinas is describing here, then, is the network of relations that is the Trinity. The term he uses to describe these unique relations is 'subsistent'. What he means by this is that their ground of existence is in themselves. There are no persons at each end of a relation; Father, Son and Holy Spirit are simply the relations.

Now Aquinas goes on to say that the subsistence of these relations can be explained by the fact that they are identical with the one divine substance, which itself is the ground of its own existence. The three relations subsist because they are the same as the one divine substance which itself is self-grounded. Despite the very important contribution that Aquinas makes through his demonstration that the Trinity does not consist of three 'somethings' who subsequently enter into relationships but is purely and simply a network of subsistent relations, his work suffers from its tie with the metaphysics of substance. What is required is a more dynamic understanding of the triune God.

Paul Fiddes takes up this challenge by introducing the idea of God as 'an event of relationships'.[38] He suggests that we refer to 'movements of relationship' or to 'three movements of relationship subsisting in one event'.[39] There is, of course, no way to imagine or visualize three interweaving relationships. When we think of relations we naturally picture two subjects who share in communion. The fact that we cannot picture the inner life of God is no bad thing, however. God is not simply one more being alongside all others. It is not even accurate to depict God as the Supreme Being. All such attempts to capture God's reality ultimately represent a failure to recognize that there is an infinite qualitative distinction between time and eternity (Kierkegaard). God exists in a manner that is absolutely other, and as such God is beyond objectification. The real advantage in speaking about God as 'an event of relationships', suggests Fiddes, is that it communicates the idea of participation.[40] God reaches out to us in love through Christ and in the power of the Spirit inviting us to participate in the event of the divine relations.

David Cunningham also uses the term *participation* to describe this 'event of relationships', but he uses it in a very specific way. In using this descriptor, he indicates that the divine life is first and foremost an event of mutual indwelling. Further, participation is a virtue that we humans are also called to enact. If the doctrine of the Trinity has anything to teach us about authentic existence it is that communion rather than individualism is the goal of human life. 'The focus on *participation* suggests that human beings are called to understand themselves, not as "individuals" who may (or may not) choose to enter into relationships, but rather as mutually indwelling and indwelt, and to such a degree that – echoing the mutual indwelling of the Three – all pretensions to wholly independent existence are abolished.'[41] Participation, then, is a trinitarian 'virtue' that marks our human existence. Cunningham captures this fact with the metaphor of 'paralleling'.[42] Our human life parallels in a certain sense the divine life. A careful study of human existence will reveal certain triune imprints or marks.

Triune Marks

Cunningham derived the word *mark* from the Latin *vestigium*. In the theological tradition of the *vestigia trinitatis*, there is an attempt to identify parallels in human experience to the triune life of God. In *De Trinitate*, Augustine presents a large number of threefold *vestigia*: the lover, the beloved and love; the mind, its knowledge and its love; memory, understanding and will; man, woman and child; and a host of others.

We need to be clear about what Cunningham means when he uses the term *mark*. He is not saying, for instance, that God has placed little pieces of divinity in the world.[43] This would amount to a kind of pantheism. Neither is Cunningham implying that a *vestige* refers to a mark of something that is no longer present.[44] On this view, God has created the world and then left us to it. Our task then becomes to discern the divine imprints left behind. What Cunningham wants to convey with his use of the word *mark* is the notion of 'presence-in-absence'.[45] God is invisible to us but nevertheless continues to have an influence. God is actively interested and personally involved in the world.

As I have just indicated, Augustine's *vestigia trinitatis* approach is the primary source of inspiration for Cunningham. A vitally important image for Augustine is the three psychological faculties of memory, understanding and will. These are distinct and yet there is a mutual indwelling. The interrelationship exists because there is a 'mutual comprehension', and this mutual comprehension in turn indicates a fundamental equality between the faculties.

> Whatever of intelligible things that I do remember and will, it follows that I also understand. My will also comprehends my whole understanding and my whole memory, if only I make use of the whole of what I understand and remember. Wherefore, when all are mutually comprehended by each one, and are comprehended as wholes, then each one as a whole is equal to each other as a whole, and each one as a whole is equal to all together as wholes; and these three are one life, one mind, and one essence.[46]

Now some theologians believe that far from shedding light on the nature of the trinitarian relations, the search for the *vestigia* is quite unhelpful and even dangerous. Barth's fundamental concern is that the search for images of the Trinity constitutes an elevation of reason over revelation.[47] What is construed as interpretation ('saying *the same thing* in other words') is in reality illustration ('saying the same thing *in other words*'). What begins as an attempt to shed light on the doctrine of the Trinity ends in a neglect of the centrality of God's Word. All the data we need to guide us in constructing our theology of the Trinity, argues Barth, may be found in the biblical narratives. Gunton concurs with the general thrust of this objection, pointing out that the flow of illumination when using the *vestigia* can too easily be established as from world to God rather than the other way round.[48] However, it is also clear that Gunton is not opposed to the idea of the marks *per se*. He engages in an attempt to find an analogy between the relational structure in the created order and the perichoretic relationships in the Trinity. In providing a warrant for this approach he writes: 'If God is God, he is the source of all being, meaning and truth. It would seem reasonable to suppose that all being, meaning and truth is, even as created and distinct from God, in some way marked by its relatedness to its creator.'[49] As long as the position of revelation is not compromised, Gunton is happy to work with trinitarian analogies.

Against Barth's objection, Cunningham argues that while the primacy is clearly with revelation, we do need to attend to the question of how we *receive* God's truth.[50] That is, the narratives pointing to the doctrine of the Trinity do not simply speak for themselves. We need to find the tools that can help us in our task of hearing and understanding. The set of psychological images developed by Augustine is one such tool. The *vestigia* do not and cannot produce wholly new knowledge, but they can and do help us understand more fully what has already been made known to us through the scriptural narratives.

Clearly, the question of the validity of the *vestigia* is a complex one. It has been possible to identify only one major objection to the use of the idea of triune imprints, and to offer the outline of what I take to be an adequate response. Since I shall make significant use of the idea throughout this book, I hope that I have said enough to indicate that it is possible to use the notion of triune marks without compromising the primacy of revelation.

Summary

What I have been trying to do is to sketch the outlines of some recent attempts to point up the practical nature of the doctrine of the Trinity, and in the process to identify the themes that will be developed in the rest of this book. In the older theologies, the triune God was presented as locked up inside itself. Those who have been at the forefront of the renewal of the doctrine of the Trinity, however, have focussed on the Trinity as an open fellowship of love that invites humans to share in its communion. While fully acknowledging the value in this relational approach, theologians such as David Cunningham point out that the notion of paralleling is another way of developing the practical dimension in trinitarian theology. There are triune marks in human existence. These imprints of the divine point to the kind of life that humans are called to live.

Notes

1   This is the way Ted Peters characterizes scepticism over the relevance of the doctrine of the Trinity. See his *God as Trinity: Relationality and Temporality in Divine Life* (Louisville, Ky.: Westminster/John Knox Press, 1993), p. 28.
2   C.M. LaCugna, *God for Us: The Trinity and the Christian Life* (HarperSanFrancisco, 1991), p. 1.
3   See, for example, D. Cunningham, *These Three Are One: The Practice of Trinitarian Theology* (Oxford: Blackwell, 1998), Ch. 3.

4   See J. Moltmann, *The Trinity and the Kingdom of God* (London: SCM Press, 1981), Ch. 1. Moltmann contrasts these notions of God with a trinitarian conception.

5   For a discussion on the way God as supreme substance is situated in Greek philosophy and religion, see Moltmann, *The Trinity*, p. 10ff.

6   Ibid., p. 11.

7   P. McEnhill and G. Newlands, *Fifty Key Christian Thinkers* (London: Routledge, 2004), p. 27.

8   Ibid., p. 27.

9   See ibid., p. 36.

10 See S. Grenz, *Rediscovering the Triune God: The Trinity in Contemporary Theology* (Minneapolis: Fortress Press, 2004), p. 8.

11 See ibid., p. 8.

12 Moltmann, *The Trinity*, p. 13.

13 See ibid., p. 13.

14 Ibid., p. 15.

15 See K. Rahner, *The Trinity*, trans. J. Donceel (London: Burns and Oates, 1970).

16 Ibid., p. 35.

17 Ibid., p. 37.

18 See ibid., p. 37.

19 Moltmann, *The Trinity*, p. 156.

20 J. Moltmann, *History and the Triune God* (New York: Crossroad, 1992), p. 60.

21 See LaCugna, *God for Us*, p. 247.

22 See ibid., p. 288ff.

23 Peters, *God as Trinity*, p. 15.

24 LaCugna, *God for Us*, p. 289.

25 Ibid., p. 290.

26 Ibid., p. 304.

27 See ibid., p. 230.

28 Rahner, *The Trinity*, p. 22.

29 See LaCugna, *God for Us*, p. 222.

30 Ibid., p. 229.

31 Ibid., pp. 223–4.

32 See Grenz, *Rediscovering the Triune God*, p. 162.

33 J. Thompson, *Modern Trinitarian Perspectives* (Oxford University Press, 1994), p. 28.

34 This is Colin Gunton's point. See his 'The God of Jesus Christ', *Theology Today* 54:3 (1997), pp. 325–34.

35 Ibid., p. 329.

36 See Cunningham, *These Three Are One*, Ch. 2.

37 See Aquinas, *Summa Theologiae*, Ia.2.1–5. I have used the edition trans. by T. Gilby (London: Eyre & Spottiswoode, 1964–5).

38 See P. Fiddes, *Participating in God: A Pastoral Doctrine of the Trinity* (London: Darton, Longman and Todd, 2000), p. 36ff.

39 Ibid., p. 36.

40 See ibid., p. 37.

41 D. Cunningham, 'Participation as a Trinitarian Virtue', *Toronto Journal of Theology* 14:1 (1998), pp. 7–25 (p. 10).

42 See Cunningham, *These Three Are One*, Ch. 3.

43 See ibid., p. 91.

44 See ibid., p. 92.

45 Ibid., p. 93.

46   Augustine, *The Trinity*, trans. S. McKenna (Boston: St Paul Editions, 1965), pp. 200–201.

47   See K. Barth, *Church Dogmatics*, I.1. 8.3: *Vestigium Trinitatis* (Edinburgh: T. & T. Clark, 1936).

48   See C. Gunton, *The Promise of Trinitarian Theology* (Edinburgh: T. & T. Clark, 1991), p. 121, n. 18.

49   C. Gunton, *The One, the Three and the Many* (Cambridge University Press, 1993), p. 167.

50   See Cunningham, *These Three Are One*, p. 100.

PART I
TRINITY AND THE GENERAL MINISTRY OF CARE

MANAGING RELATIONAL SPACE

Chapter 2

Pastoral Care as Polyphony

Polyphony is a musical term which denotes the simultaneous singing or playing of two or more melodic lines that fit together as equally important parts in the overall structure of a piece. In the previous chapter, we encountered David Cunningham's notion of marks or imprints of the Trinity. Polyphony is one such mark. In relation to the triune God, polyphony refers to the way in which simultaneous difference exists as a homogeneous unity. Cunningham contends that we find the same dynamic at work in human life. Our existence is marked or imprinted with this central trinitarian characteristic.

In this chapter, I shall follow Cunningham's lead and make the suggestion that polyphony is an imprint of the triune God in the ministry of care. That is, authentic pastoral relationships constitute a reflection or a paralleling of the polyphonic relationality in the Godhead. While there are a number of polyphonic categories that could be developed, and some of these will be briefly mentioned below, we will concentrate on two sets: *wisdom* and *folly*, and *communion, nearness* and *distance*.

Alastair Campbell's pastoral image of the wise fool is both unusual and deeply illuminating.[1] Campbell points to the circus clown as an example of wise folly. Amongst the circus professionals he or she appears as an amateur, and yet his or her spontaneous and carefree escapades are the result of careful training and planning. In our pastoral visitation we do not have the sophisticated structures of the psychotherapist to carry with us, but yet in our unstructured, sometimes light, sometimes deep conversations – when they are helpful – we employ a great deal of skill and we need considerable wisdom. We need the wisdom to join with the other in *managing the space* well.

The idea of 'personal space' is one that Colin Gunton develops in his trinitarian reflections.[2] The persons in the Godhead need space to be (there is differentiation in the one God), and so do the humans created in the divine image. When there is a compression of the interpersonal space there is a failure to respect otherness. Too much space, on the other hand, means that there is no possibility of communion (the problem of individualism).

Taking our cue from Gunton's analysis, I will be suggesting that effective pastoral visitation involves a polyphony of *communion, nearness* and *distance*. We usually think of communion with the other in terms of drawing near. Empathic relating involves an attempt to close the interpersonal space. We think and feel ourselves into the inner spaces of the other. Communion cannot be sustained, however, in the absence of due regard for appropriate distance. The other needs 'space to be'. We need the wisdom and discernment to be able to read the signs well and to judge when to move in and when to pull back.

Polyphony is one of three 'marks' discussed by Cunningham (the other two are *participation* and *particularity*). Since it is the central term we will be using, it is well to begin by describing it more fully.

Polyphony and Trinity

The chief attribute of this musical term is 'simultaneous, non-excluding difference: that is, more than one note is played at a time, and none of these notes is so dominant that it renders another mute'.[3] Cunningham goes on to suggest that a theological perspective informed by polyphony would challenge any view that claims that any two contrastive categories must necessarily work against each other. He is putting in a plea for the avoidance of false dichotomies in theology. In such dichotomous thinking, increased attention to one category is seen to necessarily imply decreased attention to its contrastive partner. This he refers to as the 'zero-sum game'.[4] In this theological game, a greater emphasis on the humanity of Christ must diminish the divinity of the Word; a focus on divine immanence necessarily leads to a downplaying of God's transcendence; and so on. Those who avoid playing the 'zero-sum game' will find that they are able 'to think in terms of simultaneous difference that need not be synthesized into a single, homogeneous unity'.[5]

An example of this polyphonic thinking can be found, suggests Cunningham, in the relationship between action and passion in God.[6] When God is active there is an expression of divine sovereignty and freedom, but at the same time God demonstrates passivity through a submission to the actions of others. Action and passion in God, then, are like two notes played simultaneously in a piece of music. When God acts there is no constraint on the divine action, and yet God enters into relationships with human beings. This willingness to engage with humankind indicates a corresponding willingness to be 'moved' by us. Cunningham contends that the whole of Jesus's life manifests this dialectic of action and passion:

> At times he is supremely active, narrating the nature of God's Reign, embodying that Reign through exorcisms and healings. At other times he is clearly acted upon: he is given birth, raised in a Jewish home, questioned by the religious leaders of the day, driven away by angry crowds, and – most obviously – arrested, interrogated, tried, stripped, mocked, and crucified. That the incarnate God can be 'acted upon' by human beings in this way is a testimony to the polyphony of action and passion in God.[7]

In relation to the doctrine of the Trinity, the fundamental polyphonic categories are unity and difference. The task of the early church fathers was to defend against assaults on one or other of the two poles. Arius and Eunomius, for example, developed notions that undermined the coequality and coeternity of the Three. Since the Son was born, argued Arius, there was 'a time when he was not', while Eunomius was of the view that 'there is the Supreme and Absolute Being, and another Being existing by reason of the First, but after It though before all others; a third Being not ranking with either of these, but inferior to the one, as to its cause, to the other, as to the energy which produced it'.[8] According to this view, there is a hierarchy in the Godhead with the Father at the top as the Supreme Being, the Son a rung down, and the Spirit a further rung down. Sabellius, for his part, undermined the distinctions in the Godhead. According to him, the one divine substance manifests itself in three modes. This substance metamorphoses itself, as the need arises, to act in the mode of the Father, or of the Son, or of the Holy Spirit.[9]

In their responses to these challenges, the key category for the Cappadocian Fathers was relation. The three persons of the Trinity exist in a perfect communion. In this communion, there is no severance or division: 'He who receives the Father virtually receives at the same time both the Son and the Spirit.'[10] Basil is here upholding the unity in the Trinity. He is careful, though, to hold this in proper tension with the distinctiveness of the Three. There is a 'proper peculiarity of the Persons delivered in the faith, each of these being distinctively apprehended by His own notes'.[11] Three persons in communion is the summary line in the Cappadocian approach.

The category of relation is also central in Thomas Aquinas's trinitarian theology. For Aquinas, God is Being-Itself. Thus, the nature of God is To-Be. 'In *De Deo Trino*', writes LaCugna, '[Aquinas] shows that the To-Be of God is To-Be-Related. Thus, while God may be the supremely actual and simple existent, this existence is personal, indeed, tripersonal, by virtue of the differentiation of divine persons in relation to each other.'[12] The starting point for Thomas in developing his understanding of God as the To-Be-Related, as we saw in the previous chapter, is the two processions in God.[13] These are the procession of the Word, which Aquinas calls generation or begetting, and the procession of Love, which he refers to as 'spiration' ('breathing out'). These processions, in turn, imply four 'real' relations: begetting, being begotten, breathing out and being breathed.[14] There are, however, only three unique relations, because the actions through which the Word and the Spirit are produced (begetting and breathing out respectively) are of the same general type. Thus the three unique relations are begetting (which includes breathing out), being begotten and being breathed forth. These unique relations are called 'subsistent' to indicate that the ground of their existence is in themselves.

While there is no consensus on how exactly to interpret the idea of *person*, everyone is agreed that it does not refer to a centre of consciousness. There are not three entities in the Trinity, each operating out of its own particular consciousness. Rather – as Aquinas's use of the term 'subsistent' indicates – there are simply three relations. These relations indwell each other in a communion of love. The intimate communion they share in constitutes their unity; the unique nature of each relation indicates their particularity.

The Trinity is a polyphony in which three distinctive notes are sounded without any one note muting any other. We need now to inquire as to the role of polyphony in pastoral care.

Polyphony and Pastoral Care

Pastoral care is a demanding and subtle ministry because of its polyphonic nature. The caregiver needs an interpersonal style in which contrastive qualities are held together in a homogeneous manner. Alastair Campbell has provided us with three central images for pastoral ministry. Many theorists and practitioners of pastoral care have found them extremely helpful. What I find especially interesting is the fact that the way in which Campbell develops his images points very clearly to the polyphonic nature of the ministry of care. He refers to the *toughness* and the *tenderness* of the shepherd, to the *woundedness* and the *health* of the wounded healer, and to the *wisdom* and *folly* in the wise fool. I shall discuss the first two images briefly, but it is the third, and less well-known, image that I want to concentrate on.

The shepherd image is of course a traditional one. Shepherds in the ancient Near East expressed a tender care for their sheep, but they also needed a hardness to survive. Given the climatic conditions of Palestine, shepherding was a strenuous and hazardous occupation. When the weather was dry, it was necessary to move the sheep over long distances in search of greener pastures and more ample supplies of water. While on the move, the shepherd had to contend with the threats from robbers and wild beasts. To be sure, he needed to care gently for his flock, but he also needed to be robust enough to deal with the attacks of human and beast. Campbell puts it this way:

> We can see at once that there is a mixture of tenderness and toughness in the character of the shepherd. His unsettled and dangerous life makes him a slightly ambiguous figure – more perhaps like the cowboy of the 'Wild West' than the modern shepherd in a settled farming community, yet loving and caring at the same time.[15]

Campbell is not, of course, advocating a 'tough guy' or 'tough gal' approach in pastoral care. What he is pointing to is a need for a virtuosity that reflects that of Jesus. He was one who sounded notes of both tough courage and gentle love, and so must his under-shepherds.

While those of us in the pastoral ministry have sometimes thought of our frailty, vulnerability and hurts as liabilities, the image of the wounded healer says to us that these dimensions of our humanity can be resources for us. Campbell reminds us, though, that wounding in and of itself is not a power in bringing healing to others. It is only when we have found hope in shadow experiences that we are able to bring some light through our presence. 'Wounded healers heal because they, to some degree at least, have entered the depths of their own experiences of loss and in those depths found hope again.'[16]

We are by now very familiar with these images of shepherd and wounded healer (although Campbell brings a freshness through his interpretation). But the third image is less well known to us. An important dimension in pastoral care, according to Campbell, is indicated by 'the dishevelled, gauche, tragic-comic figure of the fool'.[17] His description of this character is multi-faceted. I will concentrate only on the two elements that are most relevant to our current concerns, namely, the simplicity in folly and the folly of the clown.

In order to draw out the simplicity in the figure of the wise fool, Campbell begins with the thinking of Erasmus in *Praise of Folly*.[18] The simpleton or 'natural fool' in medieval times was contrasted with the 'artificial fool', the court jester. Natural fools lack the capacity for reasoning. They have very little knowledge to work with and they cannot penetrate the subtleties and complexities that characterize the relationships of others around them. But this lack of sophistication, observes Campbell, results in a 'refreshing directness' in their engagement with other people. The wisdom in the simplicity is that it exposes pomposity, insincerity and self-deception.

Now of course we cannot pretend to the simplicity of the natural fool. When we attend to this image, however, we are able to strip away some of the layers of 'adult wisdom' that hold us back from honest, straightforward relating. Simplicity in our engagement with others means a higher level of spontaneity and directness. It also means that it allows us to draw near to the other. The verbosity of sophisticated conversation is a liability for us. 'We use words to distance ourselves from experience – our own and other people's – and so lose the simple sense of *nearness* – nearness of nature, of other people and of God.'[19]

The natural fool is one source of learning for us; the circus clown is another.[20] Campbell draws on Heije Faber's insights in *Pastoral Care in the Modern Hospital*.[21] Faber compares the way a minister operates in a hospital setting to the work of a circus clown. The analogy with the clown can be established on three fronts: he is one of many circus acts, yet he has his own unique role; he presents as an amateur in the midst of a troupe of highly trained professionals; and his act is one of creative spontaneity yet it is possible only because of careful preparation and training. Campbell suggests that this analogy can be taken to apply to pastoral care as a whole: 'Pastoral care must avoid the temptation to turn its "clown act" into the polished performance of the trapeze artiste, the lion tamer, or the juggler. The folly, the scandal of pastoral care, is that it describes the stumbling efforts of the non-professional to care for others.'[22]

Campbell is not simply making excuses for 'dedicated incompetence' in the pastoral ministry. Caregivers need a high level of training and preparation to be effective. The clown, after all, may appear to be stumbling in a carefree manner from one uproarious escapade to the next, but we know that each step in the act has been assiduously prepared for. Like the clown, we are amateurs who use a high level of skill. We need the wisdom and the virtuosity to sound a range of notes in our pastoral engagements that all blend together. Toughness mixed with tenderness, woundedness and health, and a folly that is also wise: these notes need to be expertly played in the polyphony of care.

A Case of Wise Folly

Andrew Lester recounts an experience from his pastoral ministry that illustrates well the 'clown act' that Campbell suggests is pastoral care. It concerns a visit to a little girl in hospital.

> This week I made an initial pastoral call to meet six-year-old Candice, who was in hospital with a serious intestinal blockage. The nurse told me that Candice was usually verbal and felt well enough that day for conversation. However, when I tried to begin a dialogue she looked down at her bed or at the far wall. For several minutes, I tried every 'trick' I knew, all in vain. She was uncomfortable, caught off guard in some manner. Finally, I bid a weak, and frustrated, good-by, indicated that I would return later, and retreated in defeat.[23]

When Lester returned, he tried a different approach. He brought along his puppet, Fuzzy. Fuzzy performed the role of taking the attention off Candice, and helping her relax and gain confidence. The initial conversation was between Lester and Fuzzy. Fuzzy 'inquired' as to why Candice was in hospital. He went on to ask questions about the medical devices being used, such as the intravenous tube. Finally, he asked if the entry needle for the IV was causing Candice pain. To which Lester replied, 'I don't know. You'll have to ask Candice.' In this way, the little girl was gently brought into the conversation.

Many of us will be able to relate very closely to Lester's initial experience. We come to a pastoral encounter with a relatively high level of theological and pastoral sophistication and sometimes it all seems to count for nothing. In a word, we feel naked. Naked and ashamed we slink off. Lester walked away embarrassed, but to his credit he came back to try again. In order to make a connection with Candice, he needed to let go, to do some shedding. He needed to let go of the 'adult wisdom', to lose his 'bag of tricks' for snaring the attention of a child, in order to enter into the simplicity of play. Lester had to shed the feeling that playing with puppets is foolish and join in the folly of Fuzzy.

To become a skilled puppeteer is not the point. Indeed, the more expert the performance the greater the risk that the act of pastoral care will fail. Lester's aim was not to entertain Candice, but rather to draw near to her in her experience of illness and hospitalization. Others come into the hospital with talented performances to brighten the day of the children. But Lester wants to meet Candice, to come close to her, and his amateur skills are enough. The focus is not on the clever way he uses Fuzzy, but rather the puppet provides a soft focus for the pastoral relationship. Such is the simplicity and the virtuosity of the caregiver. This soft focus is made possible through the creation of space. While Candice is attending to Fuzzy, there is a safe distance between her and Lester. The puppet is used by Lester to close the space at a pace that feels comfortable for Candice.

Co-managing the Space

The idea of space and of achieving the right kind of space is critical in pastoral relationships. Space is also a key category in trinitarian theology, as Colin Gunton shows. In his essay 'The Human Creation: Towards a Renewal of the Doctrine of the *Imago Dei*',[24] Gunton wants to go beyond the approach to the *imago* that centres on reason. He is aiming for a relational ontology – something that is unachievable if rationality is the focus. A stress on reason 'encourages the belief that we are more minds than we are bodies, with all the consequences that has: for example, in creating a non-relational ontology, so that we are cut off from each other and from the world by a tendency to see ourselves as imprisoned in matter'.[25]

Gunton uses the category of space to help shape his relational ontology. This space, however, needs to be correctly defined. If there is too much space in the relational sphere there is a fall into individualism. Mutual participation in relationships implies nearness. Too little space, on the other hand, is also a problem. When the other sits on top of me, so to speak, I lose my freedom. She fails to make room for me and so shows a lack of respect for my otherness.

In developing his theological anthropology, Gunton picks up on the notion of the Greek theologians that God is a communion of persons. Each person is distinct and yet the Three indwell each other and so share in an essential unity. A close look at this understanding of the Trinity, suggests Gunton, will provide us with the right conceptualization of relational space.

> We have a conception of *personal space*: the space in which three persons are for and from each other in their otherness. They thus confer particularity upon and receive it from one another. That giving of particularity is very important: it is a matter of space to be. Father, Son and Spirit through the shape – the *taxis* – of their inseparable relatedness confer particularity and freedom on each other. That is their personal being.[26]

Gunton picks up the relational cues here to shape his anthropology. We are created in the image of God and it is therefore to be expected that relationality will be fundamental to our humanity. That is to say, if God is a communion of persons involving mutual participation, we will experience our humanity in our relatedness to others.

The structure or *taxis* of human community is a relationality that involves both participation (nearness) and otherness (distance). The space between us has to be the right kind of space: we need 'the space to be'. 'To be a person is to be constituted in particularity and freedom – to be given space to be – by others in community. *Otherness* and *relation* continue to be the two central and polar concepts here. Only where both are given due stress is personhood fully enabled.'[27] In other words, relationality is polyphonic. We need to play the notes of otherness and participation in harmony if we are to establish the right kind of relational space.

The aim in pastoral relationships is to draw near to the other person. There is always an interpersonal gap because she is she and I am I. There are two inner worlds involved in an encounter with another person. As John Savage puts it, 'This gap is a result of trying to interface between two worlds. One is the external world that I perceive through my senses. The second is the inner world of my brain, where I must constantly interpret both that which is going on inside me, as well as attempting to bridge the gap that occurs when I try to make contact with the outside world.'[28] I try to close this gap through empathy. I want to think and feel myself into her inner universe. At the same time, I need to give the other space to be. It is judging when to move in close and when to make some room that is a central art in pastoral relationships. It could be said that this pastoral art requires a capacity to play a polyphony – a polyphony of *communion, nearness* and *distance*. We usually associate communion with coming close to the other, but unless there is also appropriate distance there cannot be a real meeting between us. Communion is established when two people are able to draw near while at the same time making space for otherness.

I went to see Ruth at the request of one of my parishioners, Joan. The two had met at an ecumenical bible study. Joan had observed that Ruth was finding it very difficult to cope with the multiple sclerosis from which she was suffering and asked her if she would like a visit from me. On my first visit to Ruth's home we had spent about half an hour getting to know each other when I decided that it might be time to raise the issue of her illness. She had been talking about a friend who had been having some personal problems, and I took the opportunity to provide an opening for her to talk, saying: 'And you have been having a real struggle with your MS.' Up to this point, Ruth had seemed very comfortable with me. I felt that there was a good rapport developing. What happened in that instant took me totally by surprise. Ruth froze up completely. Her face went blank and she simply stared, making no response at all. I realized immediately, of course, that I had moved in too close too quickly. I remember feeling shame. I felt that I had violated Ruth in some way.

Reflecting on the experience, I wonder if there was something else happening other than the fact that I had misjudged Ruth's readiness to talk about her personal struggle. Gunton interprets 'personal space' as making room for otherness. Providing personal space is allowing the other to be herself, to be the fullness of her personhood. Perhaps part of the reason Ruth felt assaulted by me is that my lead-in comment was perceived by her as an attempt to shrink her personhood to within the bounds of her disease. It goes without saying that this was not my intention. I was attempting to move in close to the pain of her personal struggle; I wanted to be able to make an empathic connection with her experience of her illness. But she experienced something else. It felt to her as though the expansive space in which she lives and moves was being shrunk down.

What transpired over the next few weeks seems to confirm this interpretation of my failure in negotiating the interpersonal space. After the sudden and dramatic breakdown in the rapport between us, I quickly shifted back to safe ground. To my great relief, Ruth seemed to recover her composure and was quite happy to talk with me again. Nevertheless, at the end of our time together it took some courage to suggest that I might return. Over the next four visits we talked about her family, about her former career, about her interests, about everything except her disease. I must say that it felt a little strange, given that I had been invited to come because she needed someone to talk to about living with MS. The only mention in those weeks came in an oblique form in the prayer at the end of our time together. I decided however that I should not raise the issue, but rather wait upon Ruth. Finally on the fifth visit it all came tumbling out. We had been chatting for a while when Ruth excused herself. She came back with a pile of literature on MS and talked very freely about the disease and how it was affecting her and her family.

A very deep pastoral bond developed between Ruth and me. She began attending my church and over the next two years we got to know each other very well. Indeed, a lovely friendship developed between us. Out of our struggle to manage the space between us, in my sometimes stumbling efforts to move near and to make some room, there came an experience of communion.

Summary

The trinitarian virtue of polyphony is mirrored, I have argued, in effective pastoral care. Just as the divine communion exists in and through polyphony, so too pastoral relationships require the capacity to sound polyphonic notes. In the pastoral ministry we need the virtuosity to hold together toughness and tenderness, woundedness and health, wisdom and folly, and nearness and distance.

In our reflections, the last of these polarities was especially important. Joining with the other in managing the interpersonal space is a crucial skill for pastoral caregivers. We aim in our pastoral relationships to establish communion through drawing near, but we also need to make room for others. If the ministry of care were only about learning how to move in close it would be challenging enough. However, what makes it especially demanding is that at the same time we need to give the other person space to be, room to be herself. Communion, nearness and distance are the categories in the Trinity that take us to the heart of pastoral relationality.

Notes

1   See A. Campbell, *Rediscovering Pastoral Care*, 2nd edn (London: Darton, Longman and Todd, 1986), Ch. 5.
2   See C. Gunton, *The Promise of Trinitarian Theology* (Edinburgh: T. & T. Clark, 1991), Ch. 6.
3   D. Cunningham, *These Three Are One: The Practice of Trinitarian Theology* (Oxford: Blackwell, 1998), p. 128.
4   Ibid.
5   Ibid., p. 131.
6   See ibid., pp. 142–3.
7   Ibid., p. 143.
8   Gregory of Nyssa records this as Eunomius's view. See his *Against Eunomius*, Book I, in *A Select Library of Nicene and Post-Nicene Fathers*, vol. 5 (Grand Rapids, Mich.: Eerdmans, 1988), p. 50.
9   See Basil the Great, *The Nine Homilies of the Hexaemeron and the Letters*, in *A Select Library of Nicene and Post-Nicene Fathers*, vol. 8 (Grand Rapids, Mich.: Eerdmans, 1978), pp. 251, 254.
10 Ibid., p. 139.
11 Ibid.
12 C.M. LaCugna, *God for Us: The Trinity and Christian Life* (HarperSanFrancisco, 1991), p. 153.
13 See Thomas Aquinas, *Summa Theologiae*, Ia.27.1–5. I have used the edition trans. by T. Gilby (London: Eyre & Spottiswoode, 1964–5).
14 See Aquinas, *Summa*, Ia.28.4.
15 Campbell, *Rediscovering Pastoral Care*, p. 27.
16 Ibid., p. 43.
17 Ibid., p. 47.
18 See ibid., p. 49ff.
19 Ibid., p. 61.
20 See ibid., p. 58ff.
21 H. Faber, *Pastoral Care in the Modern Hospital* (Philadelphia: Westminster Press, 1971).
22 Ibid., p. 59.
23 A. Lester, *Pastoral Care with Children in Crisis* (Philadelphia: Westminster Press, 1985), p. 86.
24 See Gunton, *The Promise*, pp. 104–21.
25 Ibid., p. 105.
26 Ibid., p. 113.
27 Ibid., p. 117.
28 J. Savage, *Listening and Caring Skills in Ministry* (Nashville, Tenn.: Abingdon Press, 1996), p. 11.

Chapter 3

Hospitality in Pastoral Ministry

The theme that we are developing in this first part of the book is *managing the space*. As we saw in the previous chapter, a central feature of trinitarian life is the way in which the space between the divine persons is 'managed'. On one level, the fact that they share life fully in the harmony of perfect love means that they draw as near as possible to each other. Perfect giving and receiving in love means that the relational space is contracted to a point. There are no gaps for misunderstanding, animosity and selfishness to work their way into. On another level, though, space needs to be opened up in order for the Three to express their particularity. If there were no space to be in the Trinity the distinctions between the three persons would collapse. In what follows, the notion of communal space and, more particularly, the management of that space will be used to cast light on two important pastoral issues. The first is the practice of hospitality, and the second is the relationship between acceptance and confrontation.

To offer hospitality to another person is to create a space in which she feels welcome, 'at home'. A guest feels at home when she is allowed to be truly herself. Beyond adhering to the commonly accepted rules of good behaviour, she does not have to act in a certain way in the company of the host to be accepted by him. She is given the freedom to come as she is.

Beyond being at home in someone else's space is the bigger reality of being at home in the world. The Christian community believes that to be at home in the world one must live according to the vision of the Realm of God. Jesus came into the world to invite others to share in the life of God's Realm. We might say that he came as the ultimate expression of the hospitality of God. A primary characteristic of Jesus's ministry was its radical openness. The call to life in God's community was given to *all* people. Life in the Realm of God is not just for the righteous, for the privileged, for those with status and power; it is for all. People are invited to come as they are to receive God's grace. However, there are also limits to the hospitality of God. Those who share in the life of the community of God are called to live in conformity to Christ. There is both unbounded and bounded openness in the hospitality of God.

I want to suggest that this dialectic of openness and limitation is central in relation to pastoral ministry. Openness to the other is fundamental in a pastoral relationship. In counselling theory this is articulated through the concept of acceptance or unconditional positive regard. To be acceptant of the other, though, does not mean that one must condone all her attitudes, values and behaviours. The theory of acceptance makes room for a challenge to values and actions that militate against health and well-being. In a pastoral perspective, challenge involves calling the other to live faithful to Christ and his way of life.

I will begin our discussion by pointing up the trinitarian structure in the hospitality of God. The use of the hospitality image in understanding the nature of pastoral work will then be explored. In so doing, we will take our lead from divine hospitality and its dialectic of openness and limitation.

The Hospitality of God

When we think of hospitality our minds turn to guests, preparing the home and providing meals. Our preparations and our hosting gestures are designed to help the guest feel at home. The scripture scholar Brendan Byrne highlights the fact that a significant portion of Jesus's ministry is shaped around sharing meals and offering hospitality in general: 'Hospitality, in a variety of expressions, forms a notable frame of reference for the ministry of Jesus.'[1] Byrne goes on to show how we can take this further. In the gospels, Jesus is presented as the visitor from God calling others into a new experience of life in God's community. We are faced, then, with a question: How will this visitor, this guest, be received? What is crucial here is that those who receive him are brought into a much wider circle of hospitality, namely the 'hospitality of God'. 'The One who comes as visitor and guest in fact becomes *host* and offers a hospitality in which human beings and, potentially, the entire world, can become truly human, be at home, can *know* salvation in the depths of their hearts.'[2]

The familiar story of Zacchaeus climbing a tree in order to see Jesus (Luke 19:1–10), suggests Byrne, provides us with a perfect model of this dynamic of Jesus's visitation as the occasion for an experience of the hospitality of God.[3] Zacchaeus suffers exclusion on two grounds. In the first place, he is short in stature and cannot see over the crowd. More significantly, he is a tax collector and therefore part of that class which is shunned by those who resent the collusion with the occupying power, Rome. Jesus, however, is beyond these exclusionary attitudes and invites himself to Zacchaeus's home (v. 5). There he pronounces a wonderful word of healing and liberation: 'Today salvation has come to this house, because this one too is a son of Abraham' (v. 9). This, says Byrne, is a biblical way of saying, 'He's one of us; he's at home in the People of God; he's included within the community of salvation'.[4]

God sent Jesus into the world to call people into the community of salvation. The meeting between Jesus and Zacchaeus is a perfect paradigm of God's hospitality. We have here a model for our communal life of inviting and welcoming. The visitation of divine healing and love that Zacchaeus experienced 'challenges the community to become more effectively a beachhead of the kingdom, where lost human beings can find welcome and new life in the grasp of a hospitable God'.[5]

Now for our purposes it is important to recognize that this extension of divine hospitality has a trinitarian structure. Christ comes in the power of the Spirit to invite people into communion with God. To be truly human is to share in communion with the Living God. Jesus comes to call people to full humanness through the offer of a saving relationship. He is both the model and the bearer of this healing and liberating communion. Jesus is the communion of the divine and the human and he reaches out to others, offering them a share in his experience. He is the link between God and humanity. It is as people conform themselves to Jesus that they are united to God.

The Holy Spirit is the enlivening power that draws all persons – divine and human – into communion. Through the Spirit's power people are freed from sin and conformed to the person of Christ. This Catherine LaCugna refers to as a 'deification' of the human: 'The Spirit deifies human beings, makes them holy, sets them free from sin, ... conforms them to the person of Christ. The deified person's way of being in relationship with self, with others, with the goods of the earth, with God, corresponds to Jesus's way of being in relationship.'[6]

Life in a community constituted by the Spirit and conformed to Christ is shaped by a radical openness and acceptance. When Christian community is functioning optimally, all those who come are welcomed and affirmed as children of God. LaCugna puts it very well:

> The goal of Christian community, constituted by the Spirit in union with Jesus Christ, is to provide a place in which *everyone* is accepted as an ineffable, unique, and unrepeatable image of God, irrespective of how the dignity of a person might otherwise be determined: level of intelligence, political correctness, physical beauty, monetary value ... The community of Jesus Christ is the one gathering place in which persons are to be accepted and valued unconditionally, as equal partners in the divine dance.[7]

Jürgen Moltmann's term for this unconditional embrace of the other is 'open friendship'.[8] Genuine friendship involves '*respect* for the other person's freedom with deep *affection* for him or her as a person'.[9] To offer 'open friendship' to another person means that one wants to share life fully with her, while at the same time granting her space to be. Moltmann holds up the person and work of Jesus as the perfect exemplar of 'open friendship'. In this way, he shows that 'open friendship' is another name for the trinitarian fellowship.[10] Human beings come to know the essence of trinitarian communion – the giving and receiving of infinite love – in and through the person and work of Jesus Christ. This unbounded self-giving in love is expressed in the way Jesus reached out to all persons, especially the marginalized:

> [Jesus] celebrated the messianic feast with the people who had been thrust out of society. In inviting joy, he opened himself for them, and respected both them and the poor, as the first children of the divine grace that creates everything afresh. He recognized their dignity as people. He bridged the gulf of their self-isolation, and did away with the social prejudice under which they suffered. Through speech and gesture, the divine 'friend of sinners and tax collectors' spread the encouraging and supportive atmosphere of open friendship among men and women.[11]

There is a radical openness in the community of God (or at least there should be). The invitation to share in the blessings of the Living God is extended to all, especially the outcasts and the sinners. But it is not the case that people who join the community are free to express any value or behaviour they wish. All *persons* are welcome, but certain *behaviours* are not. There is within God's Realm both unbounded and bounded openness.

The Openness and Limit Dialectic in God's Hospitality

A feature of Jesus's ministry, as I have said, was his invitation to all people, and especially those on the margins, to come and join in the banquet in the hall of the

Kingdom. We should, however, specify what the 'all' really refers to here. In the gospels, we find a tension in relation to the scope of Jesus's outreach. He limited himself primarily to a mission to the House of Israel. That is, Jesus's basic self-understanding is that he is the Elect One calling the Elect People to a new experience of God's blessing and God's call. It is this tension between election and hospitality that exercises Letty Russell's mind in her article 'Practicing Hospitality in a Time of Backlash'.[12] Election, she notes, can be interpreted in terms of both 'specialness' and mission. That is, the elect people can focus either on their chosenness and the associated presumption of privilege, or on the fact that they have been picked for a mission to others (they are to be 'a light to the nations'). The tendency is to focus on privilege rather than calling. It is at this point that the doctrine of election threatens the openness in God's hospitality. Election can be associated with exclusion. Chosenness can be seen as 'a divine sanction for uniformity rather than unity, and for privilege of one group rather than justice for many'.[13] The way forward, suggests Russell, is to concentrate on what Jesus, through his death and resurrection, elects us to. In Christ we are elected to an outreach of witness and service. Here she echoes Moltmann's notion of open friendship. God's hospitality 'is seen in the choice of Israel and of Jesus to take on the task of becoming a light to the nations and of serving those in need. Those who see themselves elected with Christ through faith are called to take up his lifestyle of compassion and hospitality to neighbors in need'.[14]

Those of us who are in God's community are people who have accepted the gracious invitation to share in the blessings of that community; we must now extend an invitation to those outside. All are welcome to share in God's hospitality, but, says Russell, there are certain limits.[15] She identifies three boundary markers. As we shall see, these reflect her commitment to justice and, more particularly, to Christian feminism. Obviously, her way of constructing the boundary lines is not the only available option. It has the advantage, however, of being broad enough to be inclusive, and narrow enough to maintain a genuinely Christian identity and ethos. The phrase 'Christian identity and ethos' is, of course, a loaded one. The real issue is the way in which this is construed. In my view, Russell's insistence that Christ must be at the centre of communal life, together with her requirement that all interpersonal and social relations conform to the principles of love, mutuality, equality and justice, constitutes an adequate summary of the gospel ethos. Let us now see how Russell fills out this summary statement.

The first boundary marker identified by Russell is that those who take up the invitation need to know that they are joining a community with Christ at the centre. The love and the compassion in the Church – in a word, its power for living – flows from him. A central commitment in the faith community is to draw closer to Christ. A second limit is that those who share in the life of the Church must be committed to justice for all women and men. It is not possible to extend hospitality to the 'destructive intentions' of those who wish to oppress others. Finally, there is the limit associated with a commitment to mutuality with those on the fringe. Genuine hospitality is not about one person (the privileged one) doing all the giving. A one-sided hosting of the other that ignores both the gifts she has to offer and the preferences she holds is domination.

There is openness in the community of God, but it has its limits. The invitation to share in the blessings of the Realm of God goes out to everyone; those who take up the offer, however, need to respect the core values of the gospel. This dialectic of openness and limitation, I hope to show, plays an important role in the practice of pastoral care.

Hospitality and Pastoral Care

Hospitality involves the practicalities of preparing a space and of offering food and drink. But it also involves something deeper, namely the giving of oneself. A good host is one who is attentive to her guests. This attention extends beyond checking whether their glasses need topping up. For guests to feel as though they have truly been extended hospitality it is necessary for them to receive the full attention of the host. 'People know that they are welcome when hosts share their lives and not just their skills or their place. When hosts understand hospitality as offering themselves rather than as performing a task, the relationship is much richer.'[16]

Given the crucial role of personal attentiveness in hospitality, it is to be expected that some would find here a metaphor for pastoral relationships. In *The Wounded Healer*, Henri Nouwen suggests that a hospitable presence is one that is shaped around *concentration*.[17] If we are to host another and his pain, we must pay attention to him. What stops us from doing this, of course, is our self-preoccupation. Our minds become so full of our own current concerns, random thoughts and action plans that there is no space left to receive the communications of our guest. Hospitality requires preparing a place, our home, for the one we have invited. If our guest arrives and finds instead of a ready and available space a hive of activity he will feel like an intruder. Similarly, to host the wounded one, we must clear away our 'intentions', our concerns and desires, and help him to feel welcome. 'Anyone who wants to pay attention without intention has to be at home in his own house – that is, he has to discover the center of his life in his own heart.'[18]

In order to help others feel welcome, observes Nouwen, not only does the host offer his full attention, he also creates a space in which guests feel free to be themselves (as we have also seen). 'The paradox of hospitality is that it wants to create emptiness, not a fearful emptiness, but a friendly emptiness where strangers can enter and discover themselves as created free; free to sing their own songs, speak their own languages, dance their own dances ... Hospitality is not a subtle invitation to adopt the life style of the host, but the gift of a chance for the guest to find his own.'[19]

In the framework of pastoral psychology, this action of creating a 'friendly emptiness' is expressed through the practice of acceptance. It is around this pastoral practice that confusion sometimes enters. Pastoral caregivers have been greatly influenced by the Rogerian approach and for some, perhaps many, there is uncertainty about how, on the one hand, to create the empty space in which people may truly be themselves, while, on the other, challenging them to conform their lives more closely to Christ. That is, they find it difficult to develop a pastoral practice that gives expression to the 'bounded openness' that I am advocating. Given its importance for pastoral practitioners, it will be worth spending some time looking inside the person-centred system to see if we can find a place for appropriate challenge.

A Person-Centred Approach to 'Bounded Openness'

Most, if not all, of us, observed Carl Rogers, grow up under 'conditions of worth'. The kinds of message commonly received from parents are these: 'You are worthy if you think like I do.' 'You will be worth something if you do as well at school as your sister.' And finally, 'You will show your worth if you are courageous, or assertive, or funny, or …'. In the counselling relationship, Rogers aimed to provide an environment free of conditions of worth. When both the negative and the positive attitudes and behaviours are accepted by the counsellor, a person has a chance to discover who he really is. 'It is the acceptance of both the mature and the immature impulses, of the aggressive and the social attitudes, of guilty feelings and positive expressions, which gives the individual an opportunity for the first time in his life to understand himself as he is.'[20] Does this mean that the counsellor adopts a *laissez faire* approach? Is she to condone any and all attitudes, values and behaviours expressed by the client? Person-centred counsellors would say 'no'. In order to understand acceptance properly, it is necessary to make a distinction between the behavioural acts and the inner self of the client. As Godfrey Barrett-Lennard puts it, 'To be unconditionally responsive to the experiencing person does not mean accepting all their behaviour and certainly does not imply condoning everything they do. It is not the other's actions but their self or personhood that I, as client-centered therapist, prize.'[21]

The real question is, however, what does the counsellor do when she is presented with a value or a behaviour she finds unacceptable? One option is that she simply brackets it out of the engagement in order to protect against judging or moralizing. That is, she registers a feeling of disapproval, but in the interest of offering unconditional positive regard considers that she must set it aside. Those who support this approach argue that the counsellor cannot accept the client as she is and at the same time demand that she be other.[22] But is offering a challenge to certain client behaviours really demanding that she be other? Could it not rather be construed as inviting the client to explore a part of herself with which she has lost contact? This is the line pursued by person-centred counsellor Brian Thorne.[23] Thorne contrasts a true conscience with a false one. The true conscience has the function of keeping a person in touch with 'the deepest regions of the self'; it points him or her to those decisions and actions that are congruent with 'the meaning and significance of his or her life'.[24]

Thorne's term 'the deepest regions of the self' is a suggestive one, but it cries out for elaboration. What, exactly, is this zone within the self? It clearly has a link with one's sense of identity. 'My deepest self' can be taken, I think, to be equivalent to 'my true identity'. Personal identity has been described as 'a clearly delineated self-definition comprised of those goals, values, and beliefs to which a person is unequivocally committed'.[25] Note the emphasis on values in this definition. There are a growing number of psychologists who contend that values are the primary factor in the experience of personal identity.[26] The argument is that when a person acts in accordance with her value structure she feels in touch with her core self. That is to say, living true to her deepest values leads to a sense of authenticity. A person whose words and actions are congruent with her value structure feels as though she is living out of her 'true self'.

The 'true self' is also an important theological concept. Thomas Merton sees the authentic self as the experience of union with God in Christ. To experience this loving union is to experience profound joy: 'The only true joy on earth is to escape from the prison of our own selfhood ... and enter by love into union with the Life who dwells and sings within the essence of every creature and in the core of our own souls.'[27] In drawing close to God, the Christian both comes to know the divine will and is empowered to live it out. To know God and God's will is to come to one's true self. To refuse the divine life and purpose is to contradict oneself. This self-contradiction that characterizes the false self is the result of sin, according to Merton: 'To say I was born in sin is to say I came into the world with a false self. I came into existence under a sign of contradiction, being someone that I was never intended to be and therefore a denial of what I am supposed to be.'[28] Every one of us, says Merton, is 'shadowed' by an illusory person. It is an illusion to believe that one can live outside God's will.

The role of conscience is to help us break free of the grip of illusion. Conscience calls us back to the true self; it leads us to the 'deepest regions' within. The Holy Spirit, 'the inner light of conscience', is the driving force behind this movement. But conscience should not be identified solely with the Spirit. The light of the Spirit is accompanied by the grace of Christ and the love of God. As Merton stresses over and over, to live as my true self is to live in Christ: 'I no longer live, but Christ lives in me' (Gal. 2:20). When I am lost, confused or distracted, I find my way back to the deepest regions in my soul through the grace of Christ at work in stimulating my conscience.

This grace is God's great love-gift to us. God has given us God's Son that we might live through the true self. The false self sometimes gets the upper hand. Pride, egotism and self-assertion begin to take over. God is in Christ saving us from these destructive tendencies. God is in Christ leading us away from illusion and into authenticity and self-transcendence.

While the Holy Spirit is prominent in relation to conscience, it is not solely the Spirit's province. The three divine beings each sound a distinctive note in the depths of the soul. Roderick Leupp sums it up well: 'In "good conscience" ... is in triune conscience.'[29]

We began this discussion on bounded openness in the person-centred approach with an attempt to develop an adequate understanding of acceptance. It is interesting to note that Thorne finds a link between acceptance and the positive work of the conscience. The acceptant attitude of the counsellor creates an environment in which the true conscience finds its voice. In this environment one is deeply relaxed but at the same time alive with creative energy:

I sense a great relaxation which permeates every fibre of my being. I often feel sleepy and sometimes there is a faint urge to curl up in the other person's arms. I rest awhile and then comes flooding in a wave of new energy. I feel creative and excited. I can think and feel with clarity and intensity. I do not have to worry if I appear powerful or weak, virtuous or scandalous. I am alive and on the move towards the meaning of my life. My true conscience speaks to me and I might even find the courage to obey its promptings.[30]

The true conscience is always in danger, however, of being overtaken by a false one. External authorities can be allowed to exert undue influence through internalization. The voices that intrude on us often have a parental source, but sometimes it is God's voice (or at least a distorted version of it) that we hear. God the harsh judge can make God's presence felt:

> Have you forgotten all you have ever learned? Have you not heard of the sin of egotism? How dare you spend so much time dwelling on your absurd feelings. Have you forgotten that you are a worm and no man? Have you forgotten that without me you are nothing – I could extinguish you with a flick of my fingers. How dare you inflate your self-importance. Cross out the I and take up your cross. Be concerned for others, abhor this appalling me-worship. You are on the point of falling into the clutches of a guru of the me-generation which has forgotten about sacrifice, constraint and renunciation. One step further and you are lost.[31]

A very tough taskmaster is this God! The one who takes time for introspection must learn to ignore the external voices that have the power to take her away from that place where the deep meaning and significance of her life resides.

For Thorne, then, it is in an acceptant environment that the true conscience can be heard. If he had left his reflections at this point I would have been concerned. I find here a note of undue optimism – one that is characteristic of the Rogerian approach as a whole. Rogers believed that the 'organismic' or true self would actualize itself if the right conditions were set in place. When a counsellor is consistently acceptant, empathic and genuine (the three 'core conditions'), the client finds the freedom and the support necessary for her true self to grow and to develop. The counsellor does not need to direct the process; he simply creates a favourable environment for the unfolding of the self.[32] If the client is able to get in touch with her organismic self, she will always choose values and behaviours that take her in the direction of healing and growth. The counsellor is not there to direct the client towards fulfilment, but simply to create the conditions favourable for movement in that direction. Rogers puts it this way: 'Psychotherapy is the releasing of an already existing capacity in a potentially competent individual, not the expert manipulation of a more or less passive personality. Philosophically it means that the individual has the capacity to guide, regulate, and control himself, providing only that certain definable conditions exist.'[33]

The reason why I believe that this approach is founded on undue optimism is that there are those persons who, while saying they really want to change, also harbour a desire to remain where they are. To change one's attitudes and behaviours involves hard work, honesty and risk. For some this load is too much to bear. The counsellor in this case needs to be active. He needs to challenge the person in an attempt to stimulate the change process. Thorne acknowledges this need and locates counsellor confrontation within the context of genuineness or congruence (one of the three 'core conditions' in person-centred therapy).[34] Genuineness is present in the counsellor when there is a match between his internal awareness and his communication of that awareness. When a counsellor registers a disagreement with the moral stance being communicated by the client he should acknowledge his need to share his own framework of meaning and value. Often, but not always, he will choose to communicate this framework as a challenge to the 'self-betrayal' in the client. The latter having lost touch with that deep part of the self where the real meaning and significance of her life is to be found, it is necessary to stimulate in her a desire to find it again. Being confronted with an alternative moral framework achieves this purpose.

At the start of this reflection on hospitality and pastoral care, mention was made of Nouwen's image of *the empty space*. While this is helpful in pointing up the need to allow the other freedom to be truly herself, I contend that ultimately it is not an adequate metaphor for pastoral practice. Empty space is unbounded. It is a space in which people can be free without limit. But hospitality has its limits. I therefore offer *bounded openness* as a guiding metaphor for the ministry of care. Love, respect, mutuality and justice form the boundaries in the community conformed to Christ. When persons step beyond these bounds, they need to be challenged. But no one is pretending that this is easy or painless in practice. That this is so will be amply demonstrated in the following case study. It records an experience I had in attempting to care for a group of leaders. The leadership approach of two of the leaders meant that the open space characteristic of the hospitable community had been closed off. I challenged them and the group in an endeavour to reopen it and found it to be very hard work indeed!

Openness and Boundaries: A Case Study

I had recently come to the congregation as minister and was getting to know my team of pastoral leaders. We had met for lunch and were talking informally about the dreams and hopes, along with the frustrations and concerns, that the group was experiencing. I saw the gathering as an opportunity to acquaint myself better with the leaders and to orient myself to the congregation and its ministry and mission. To my surprise, when I said that I wanted to reflect together with the Elders Council on some of the issues we were facing, one of the leaders saw it as an opportunity to launch a personal attack on a fellow Elder. Bill was clearly furious with Jack. He considered that Jack had in a particular instance attempted to undermine the leadership role that Merle, Bill's sister, had taken. Bill referred to Merle's attempt to reorganize the music ministry in the congregation. Jack had apparently reported to the Council that he had heard that most of the musicians were not happy with the proposed changes, despite Merle's contention that 'everyone was on board' with the situation. Very quickly I picked up that this was not an isolated incident. Bill and Merle had been used to 'ruling the roost' and Jack was the only one who felt strong enough to challenge their rule. As a consequence, they felt deep animosity towards him, and vice versa.

In one of the early meetings of the Elders Council, I spoke against a proposal put forward by Bill and Merle. I found myself on the receiving end of the kind of hostility I had seen directed against Jack at the initial lunchtime gathering, and felt very disappointed when the elders agreed to support the proposal. Afterwards, a small group was discussing what had happened and how upset they were over the outcome. I was flabbergasted. Not one had spoken out, and indeed they had all voted in favour of the motion. 'For heaven's sake, why didn't you say something in the meeting?' I asked in frustration. 'What, and risk Bill and Merle jumping all over us?' was the reply. The others nodded in agreement.

Clearly Bill and Merle were working outside the bounds of a community conformed to the mutuality and justice of Christ. They had to have their way and they were prepared to exert the necessary force to achieve their aim. Everything was cast in the language of winning and losing. When a particular proposal that I had brought was supported by the Council, Merle leant over to me and said, 'Well, I guess you have to win sometimes.'

Obviously the situation was untenable and I had to take action to address it. I decided to call a special meeting of the Council. I communicated to the Elders my view that we were not functioning effectively as a group and that I wanted us to meet to work through some of the issues. Everyone agreed and a date and time were set.

I wanted a free and open dialogue, but I realized that this would be very difficult, if not impossible, to achieve when most of the leaders would feel intimidated by Bill and Merle. The empty space that allows freedom of expression would simply not be there. Since there was no open domain to speak into, I needed to create one – or at least to try to do so. With this in mind, I suggested that each person be given a chance to speak without being interrupted and without being responded to. Each one was to share with the group his or her vision of how we would ideally work together, along with any blocks he or she saw in the way of that vision becoming reality. As each person spoke, I wrote up on a whiteboard the issues that were emerging. I had hoped that this process would give people the freedom and the confidence to speak out. Sadly, only Jack felt able to speak the truth. Without naming Bill and Merle (he had no need to), he said that he considered that people sometimes felt pressured into making decisions against their better judgment.

In the absence of honesty, I was quite pessimistic about what might be achieved. However, after everyone had spoken, I attended to the minor, largely unimportant, issues that had been raised, and finally moved to the real issue of bullying. Bill jumped in: 'Yeah, well I know Jack was pointing the finger at me. But you know what the real problem is. It's the culture of niceness in the church. Someone has to have the guts to back up his convictions, and I'm the man for the job.' I pointed out that there was a difference between having the courage of your convictions and pushing through a proposal by force of personality. What is needed, I suggested, was an environment where we could all speak the truth we felt without fear of reprisals. In this way we could listen to the Spirit together. Bill responded that listening to the Spirit required guts and was not about always being tame and pleasant. I agreed that on occasion there would be intensity in our conversations and that honesty and courage were required at those times. Though we seemed to be making a little progress by the end of the meeting, I was not especially hopeful. Bill and Merle were so locked into the win–lose mode of thinking that I doubted we would see significant change.

While there was definitely some improvement in the months that followed, it was not long before the old pattern of bullying returned. I arranged a number of private interviews with both Bill and Merle. We talked honestly and openly, but in the end they were defeated by a lack of a desire to give up their power. Living out a pastoral practice shaped around bounded openness is sometimes a huge challenge.

Summary

We have taken our lead in reflecting on pastoral practice from the hospitality of God. God reaches out in Christ in the power of the Spirit calling everyone to share in the blessings in God's community. Further, those who come are given the space to be truly themselves. While there is this radical openness in God's hospitality, there are also limits. Everyone is welcome, but they are not free to bring their destructive attitudes and behaviours with them. Those who share in the life of the Church are called to conform themselves to the values of love, mutuality and justice that are at the heart of Christ's teaching. God's hospitality is characterized by a dialectic of openness and limitation.

We reflected on the role this dialectic plays in pastoral care. In order to express openness it is necessary to adopt a consistently acceptant attitude. A person who experiences acceptance feels free to be herself, and the environment is created for healing and growth. Sometimes, however, the person puts blocks in the way of growth. She betrays her deepest self (Thorne) by persisting with destructive values and behaviours. In the language of pastoral theology, she has moved away from conformity to Christ and the full humanness such conformity brings. At that point the pastoral caregiver needs to offer a challenge. This challenge involves holding up an alternative framework of meaning and value, namely the one we find articulated in the gospels.

Notes

1   B. Byrne, *The Hospitality of God: A Reading of Luke's Gospel* (Sydney: St Pauls, 2000), p. 4.
2   Ibid., p. 4.
3   See ibid., p. 150ff.
4   Ibid., p. 151.
5   Ibid., p. 152.
6   C.M. LaCugna, *God for Us* (HarperSanFrancisco, 1991), p. 297.
7   Ibid., p. 299.
8   See J. Moltmann, *The Spirit of Life: A Universal Affirmation* (Philadelphia: Fortress Press, 1992), pp. 255–9.
9   Ibid., p. 255.
10 Cf. J.A. McDougall, 'The Return of Trinitarian Praxis? Moltmann on the Trinity and the Christian Life', *Journal of Religion* 83:2 (2003), pp. 177–203 (p. 197).
11 Moltmann, *The Spirit of Life*, p. 258.
12 L. Russell, 'Practicing Hospitality in a Time of Backlash', *Theology Today* 52 (1996), pp. 477–85.
13 Ibid., p. 477.
14 Ibid., p. 484.
15 See ibid., pp. 483–4.
16 C. Pohl, *Making Room: Recovering Hospitality as a Christian Tradition* (Grand Rapids, Mich.: Eerdmans, 1999), pp. 180–81.
17 See H. Nouwen, *The Wounded Healer* (Garden City, NY: Doubleday, 1972), p. 91ff.
18 Ibid., p. 92.
19 H. Nouwen, *Reaching Out* (New York: Doubleday, 1975), p. 51.

20   C. Rogers, *The Carl Rogers Reader*, ed. H. Kirschenbaum and V. Land Henderson (London: Constable, 1990), pp. 72–3.
21   G. Barrett-Lennard, *Carl Rogers' Helping System: Journey and Substance* (London: SAGE Publications, 1998), p. 100.
22   See J. Hoffman, *Ethical Confrontation in Counseling* (University of Chicago Press, 1979), p. 55.
23   See B. Thorne, *Person-Centred Counselling: Therapeutic and Spiritual Dimensions* (London: Whurr, 1991), Ch. 8.
24   Ibid., p. 118.
25   A. Waterman, 'Identity Formation: Discovery or Creation?', *Journal of Early Adolescence* 4:4 (1984), pp. 329–41 (p. 331).
26   See S. Hitlin, 'Values as the Core of Personal Identity: Drawing Links between Two Theories of Self', *Social Psychology Quarterly* 66:2 (2003), pp. 118–37.
27   T. Merton, *Seeds of Contemplation* (London: Burns and Oates, 1949, 1957), p. 8.
28   Ibid., p. 11.
29   R. Leupp, *Knowing the Name of God: A Trinitarian Tapestry of Grace, Faith and Community* (Downers Grove, Ill.: InterVarsity Press, 1995), p. 170.
30   Ibid., pp. 119–20.
31   Ibid., pp. 120–21.
32   It is interesting to note that this philosophy of non-interference has close links with Taoist teaching. In 1922, Rogers joined a small group attending an international youth conference in Peking. This contact with eastern ways of thinking was expanded as he engaged in a six-month trek through the Far East. In Taoist thought, the attitude of non-interference is fundamental. There is a natural order of things to which one must attune oneself. This attunement cannot be forced but must simply be allowed to emerge. For a discussion of the connection between Rogers's non-directive approach and Taoism, see K. Cissna and R. Anderson, 'The Contributions of Carl. R. Rogers to a Philosophical Praxis of Dialogue', *Western Journal of Speech Communication* 54 (spring 1990), pp. 125–47 (p. 129).
33   C. Rogers, 'A Theory of Therapy, Personality, and Interpersonal Relationships as Developed in the Client-Centered Framework', in S. Koch (ed.), *Psychology: A Study of a Science*, vol. 3 (New York: McGraw-Hill, 1959), p. 221.
34   See Thorne, *Person-Centred Counselling*, pp. 122–3.

Chapter 4

Community and Spiritual Friendship

In Chapter 2, we discussed the idea of closeness-with-space. It was identified as vital in constructing an adequate understanding of the relationship between the caregiver and the recipient of care. This foundational relational principle will also be prominent in our reflections here. It will be used, though, in a broader context. That context is building Christian community.

We are made for a communal life. Humans are created in the image of God. God's life is expressed through the intimate relations of Father, Son and Holy Spirit. The *imago dei* is also the *imago trinitatis*. It is not only as individual persons but also as a community that we mirror the divine life. Our life together, then, is a reflection of the mutual indwelling in love that is the Trinity.

Obviously our communal life, even when it is at its very best, can only ever be a tarnished image of the triune community. The failures in trust, goodness and self-giving that are so common in Christian relationships mean that our communal experience falls far short of the perfect giving and receiving of love that characterizes the divine life. Trinitarian relationality soars far above each and every human attempt at community, and from this lofty height offers us a model of communal life. Already a warning is sounded. Is there not a danger that in taking the Trinity as our paradigm we end up placing ourselves under impossible demands? Clearly there is. We need to set about our pastoral task of building community with a mindset that is realistic enough to take due account of human frailty, but hopeful enough to believe that God's grace is always surprising.[1]

The Trinity is a model of communal life, but it is also much more than that. We are granted the enormous privilege of participating in the divine communion. As we seek to build a communion of love here on earth, we are enriched and empowered through a sharing in the grace of Christ, the love of God and the fellowship of the Holy Spirit. The notions of Trinity as model and Trinity as empowerment will guide us as we reflect on the way in which two central trinitarian dynamics, namely *kenosis* and *perichoresis*, inform the task of building community.

Kenosis points to the fact that authentic relational life requires an emptying of the self in order to be receptive to the other. It also speaks to our relationship with God. If we are to participate in God's grace, we need to make space for divine action in our lives. *Perichoresis*, mutual indwelling, refers to the fact that there is both closeness and open space in the triune God (something with which we are by now very familiar). The divine persons form a unity in love, but if there were no distance in their relational life their particularity would be lost. Similarly, in the Christian community it is important to balance intimacy and unity with a respect for individuality and personal freedom.

Kenotic Love

Kenosis comes from the Greek verb *kenoo*, meaning 'to empty'.[2] It refers to leaving a place or deserting it, to pouring out or to making void. When *kenosis* is used in a theological context it is usually employed to express the dynamics in the incarnation. The Son emptied himself in order to take on human form. The classic text in this regard is Philippians 2:6–8. There we read that Christ Jesus,

> though he was in the form of God, did not regard equality with God as something to be exploited, but emptied himself, taking the form of a slave, being born in human likeness. And being found in human form, He humbled himself and became obedient to the point of death – even death on a cross.

We should not, however, think of *kenosis* as pertaining only to the Son. It is a trinitarian dynamic. Theologians develop this notion differently. Hans Urs von Balthasar focusses on what he calls the 'double character' of the divine love that is expressed in the cross of Christ.[3] In this love, God the Father allows the Son to take on the form of poverty and self-abandonment, and God the Son identifies with us in our sin in a loving act of obedience to the will of the Father.

In his loving sacrifice Christ takes the burden of the world's sin upon himself; but he does not load this burden onto himself. If it were the case that Christ and Christ alone took up the load of sin, the doctrine of the kenotic condition would be entirely contradicted. The notion that Christ makes space within himself to receive the burden of sin makes sense only if someone else places it on him. Balthasar poignantly observes that the truth of the situation, its absolute mystery, is that the Father chooses to place the weight of the world's sin on the Son. Christ's openness on the cross expresses his 'kenotic readiness for the will of the Father'.[4]

This means, of course, that there is also a kenotic readiness required of the Father. God 'prescribes what is absolutely opposed to God' to effect with the Son the redemption of the world.[5] Self-emptying is required of God in order to prosecute an action that is utterly foreign to God-nature. In the event of the cross we have what Balthasar refers to as the 'second and truest kenosis'.[6] The first kenotic act is creation. God empties Godself to make room for the world that is spoken into being.

Jürgen Moltmann's trinitarian theology begins with the 'first' *kenosis*.[7] He observes that the fact of *creatio ex nihilo* means that there is both a 'within' and a 'without' for God. God goes outside Godself in the creative act. In order to create something outside, God must first make space within. Here Moltmann draws on the kabbalistic doctrine of *zimsum* developed by Isaac Luria. *Zimsum* refers to the contraction within God that is required for the creation of the world to take place. Before the world was, God was the fullness of existence. There was therefore originally no *nihil*. In primordial time, all is God; there is no empty space. Luria posits the notion that God, in order to produce the space that is required for the creative act, releases a portion's of God's being. God's kenotic act results in a primal, mystical space. Without it, there could not be a creation out of nothing. For Moltmann, this primal contraction in God is a trinitarian event:

If we think about this external state of affairs, transferring it by a process of reflection to the inner relationship of the Trinity, then it means that the Father, through an alteration of his love for the Son (that is to say through a contraction of the Spirit), and the Son, through an alteration in his response to the Father's love (that is, through an inversion of the Spirit), has opened up the space, the time and the freedom for that 'outwards' into which the Father utters himself creatively through the Son. For God himself this utterance means an emptying of himself – a self-determination for the purpose of self-limitation.[8]

Moltmann goes on to show how the creation and the incarnation are connected.[9] The culmination of the creation is human beings made in the image of God. Christ is the incarnation of the Son, and in this form unites himself to us. He becomes the fullest expression of the *imago*. That Christ is the true '*ikon*' of God is manifested in a definitive manner in his passion and death. He empties himself to take on the burden of the world's sin. The divine *kenosis* – God's self-humiliation – that began with the creation is completed in the cross of Christ.

I have been trying to show with the help of Balthasar and Moltmann that *kenosis* is a trinitarian event. In the creation, in the incarnation and in the cross God empties Godself for our sake. I need at this stage to describe the role that kenotic love plays in building Christian community. *Kenosis*, I suggest, is of crucial importance in opening oneself both to others and to divine action. The two areas to be addressed, then, are authentic relationships and receptivity to grace.

Any movement towards the formation of a genuine *koinonia* begins with individuals learning to be fully present to each other. We need to learn the art of authentic conversation. Our congregational life is filled to overflowing with words. Wherever we meet – at worship, in cell groups, in youth groups and in adult fellowships – there is always a great deal of talking going on. We carry each other along in our communal activities with a buzz of verbal communication. The real question, though, is how much of this interpersonal exchange is authentic conversation, and how much is simply idle chatter?[10] When I am chattering away I am self-absorbed. I focus almost exclusively on my needs, my interests, my plans, my fears and my joys. I only half-listen to my conversation partner. Any interest I express in her life is largely motivated by a desire to be thought of as well-mannered. Chatter, driven as it is by self-concern, is incapable of producing a real meeting between persons.

A genuine dialogue can develop only when there is *kenosis*. I must empty myself of self-concern for a moment in order to hear from my conversation partner. I need to create a space, a wide space, for the other to enter. The chatterer erects a wall between herself and the one she talks with – or, more correctly, at. There may be a few holes in the wall through which a little of the other's life is allowed to leak through. An authentic engagement between two people, however, demands a gap big enough to let a full flow of life pass through.

The partners in a genuine conversation are empty. There is, of course, a destructive form of emptiness. We refer to a person as empty when she has nothing to give to others. 'It's depressing being around so and so', we say, 'she is just so empty.' Such a person is depleted of the resources of love, kindness and generosity that enrich the lives of others. Kenotic love, on the other hand, is expressive of a creative emptiness. Two individuals, each with their own unique backgrounds, interests and needs, make a space for each other and community is born.

Pastors need to make sure that they are practising the art of authentic conversation. They also need to sponsor a congregational learning project. People need to be reminded of the importance of preparing a place for the other's communication. I have sometimes preached sermons that focus on what it means to really listen to others. The feedback I have received indicates that people appreciate this kind of message. It is not something that most people usually think very much about. Further, some have pointed out that they had previously been unaware of the basic principles associated with effective listening.

The message needs to be reinforced through good modelling. Brian is a pastor and a friend of mine. Having decided at one point that he needed to develop his capacity for pastoral listening, he enrolled in Labs 1 and 2 of John Savage's programme 'Calling and Caring'. Through participating in the programme he became convinced of the importance of being fully present to others. Not only that, but he also learnt the skills necessary to support this conviction. Shortly after completing the second Lab, he went on a routine pastoral visit. At the end of the visit, his elderly parishioner said to him, 'Boy, you really listen don't you! Don't think I've ever had a minister visit me who cares so much about what I'm saying. Thank you.'

Brian created an inner space for his parishioner. Though I am not sure what happened in this particular case, my experience is that often the self-giving in pastoral contact is mutual. Certainly, the ideal for Christian fellowship is a mutual commitment to self-emptying. It might seem that if we take the kenotic love of the divine persons as our model, the norm is total selflessness. In the creation and in the cross there is complete self-abandonment for the sake of the world. There *are* times when a person is called upon to empty herself for the other without any demand or expectation that he will reciprocate. He may be so hurt and broken that he has little to give in return. What he needs at that point is a Christian friend with a love that is deep enough for her to set aside her own interests and concerns in order to be fully available to him. But this one-sided *kenosis*, I want to suggest, is not the ideal for Christian communion. The moral theologian Stephen Post rightly contends that mutual love, reciprocity, is the foundational norm for human interrelations.[11] Self-sacrifice is sometimes required of us, but it is not normative for interpersonal life. The foundational moral principle is give and take, a flow of reciprocal emptying and filling. Indeed, this is precisely the way in which the divine persons experience communion. As Geoffrey Wainwright puts it, 'the divine Persons empty themselves into each other and receive each other's fulness'.[12]

A telling example of mutual kenotic love is found in the experience of the original Focalare community.[13] This movement began during World War II in Trent, Italy, under the leadership of Chiara Lubich. Inspired by Christ's *kenosis* as represented in Philippians 2:1–11, the women in this community found that if they emptied themselves before their neighbour in order to receive her needs and sorrows, her joy and hopes, a deep communion formed. Moreover, in connecting in this way with others, they found that they were able to enter more completely into what they called 'God-Love'. It was also their experience that, when the emptying and receiving of kenotic charity was mutual, God-Love became a real presence in their midst.

When I meet another person I need to clear a space for her if I am to establish a real relationship with her. Into this space she is free to speak her joy and her sorrow, her fears and her hopes. And in return, she empties herself for me. *Kenosis* is the condition of the possibility of receptivity in interpersonal life. There is another dimension of the experience of self-emptying, though, that needs to be recognized. A genuine meeting between two people is founded not only on openness but also on self-loss. Whenever a person gives of herself there is always an element of self-diminution. Kenotic love, then, involves both a clearing out of self and a donation of time and energy.

Love is a form of work. Work is produced through an expenditure of energy. In serving another, I donate some of my energy to her. Something of my self is poured into her. In this sense, I go to work for my neighbour. Simone Weil picks up on this in her reflections on the story of the Good Samaritan. She says that of those who passed by only one turned his attention to the afflicted man lying on the side of the road. 'At the moment when [his attention] is engaged it is a renunciation ... The man accepts to be diminished by concentrating on an expenditure of energy, which will not extend his own power but will only give existence to a being other than himself.'[14]

Kenotic love is therefore a discipline. A tendency to laziness is an almost universal vice. It is sometimes the case that we simply cannot find within ourselves the commitment to the other that self-giving requires. To attend to the other in her need seems too much like hard work. It is at these times that the discipline of love must take over. In his moral theory, Immanuel Kant emphasized this fact. The fundamental moral principle for Kant is duty, and self-discipline is required in order to respond to the claims that others make on us. Unfortunately, Kant did not appreciate the central place that grace has in strengthening our resolve to care for others.[15]

If I am open to divine love, I become all the more ready for self-giving. Receptivity to God requires another kind of *kenosis*. If I am filled with self – self-reliance, self-importance, and self-concern – there is no space for grace to enter.

Roderick Leupp helpfully points out that grace is not some 'vague commodity', but rather a power that establishes communion. 'Grace', he says, 'lives in Jesus Christ and encounters the world – builds community in the world – through the Holy Spirit.'[16] Leupp draws on the insights of Hadewijch, a thirteenth-century writer, to develop this notion of trinitarian grace as the foundation of Christian fellowship. The self-communication of the triune God, says Hadewijch, infuses us with a passion for justice, a fire of love and affection, and a stream of good will:

The Father has poured out his name in powerful works, and rich gifts, and just justice. The Son has poured out his name in revelations of burning affection, in veritable doctrine, and in cordial tokens of love. The Holy Spirit has poured out his name in the great radiance of his Spirit and of his light, and in the great fullness of overflowing good will, and in the jubilation of sublime, sweet surrender on account of the fruition of Love.[17]

The authentic relationships out of which community is born are sourced by these great offerings of divine grace.

There is a variety of pastoral actions that create an opportunity for the experience of grace. None is more important than the leadership of worship. Christian liturgy and worship form us in the practices required in the establishment of authentic relationships. Worship invites us 'into the constructive dance of forming relational selves in relationship to a relational God'.[18]

When we come in a spirit of emptiness to praise God and to break open the Word, the conditions are in place for God's grace to flow into us. We begin in this way to learn the grammar of communal life.[19] The building blocks in this grammar, we have said, are receptivity, self-loss, justice, love and affection, and good will. It takes time to master a language as complicated and as intricate as the language of authentic relationality. In worship, we rehearse the vocabulary and syntax of love until they become second nature. A pressing challenge for pastors, then, is planning and executing acts of worship that effectively support this learning in the practices of relational life. Tame, comfortable worship will not do it; it is only in risky worship that people learn the language of kenotic communion. Unless people are sometimes shaken and stirred, the same old bad habits persist. Here, then, is the challenge for those of us charged with the responsibility of leading public worship. We need to be ready for risk.

The kenotic love that animates life in the triune God presents us with a rich source of inspiration and challenge in our task of building community. We now turn to an equally challenging trinitarian dynamic, namely *perichoresis*.

Perichoresis and Spiritual Friendship

The Trinity is a relational entity. However, it is the way that we construe the relational life of God that is vitally important (something with which we are now quite familiar). The triune God does not consist of three centres of consciousness sharing together in relationship. Rather, God is relational life expressed through three distinct dynamics. 'In God', writes David Cunningham, 'we find not three "somethings" with some sort of independent existence, who (at some point) "decide" to come into relation with one another. They are, rather, wholly defined by this relationality; they might best be described as "relation without remainder".'[20] The persons of the Trinity *are* because of the dynamic exchange they experience in relationship.

It was this way of thinking about the Trinity that the early Greek theologians sought to capture with the term *perichoresis*. It means 'being-in-one-another, permeation without confusion. No person exists by him/herself or is referred to him/herself'.[21] Other terms that describe this notion of being-in-one-another are interpenetration, mutual indwelling, or 'mutual reciprocal participation'.[22] The divine persons participate together in the intimacy of love and self-giving. The metaphor of dancing is commonly used to express the meaning of *perichoresis*. The Three flow together in a continuous movement of love. 'In this love the Father and the Son are intertwined like dancers moving to the music of the Spirit.'[23] There is eternal order and symmetry in this dance, but at the same time there is diversity.

The connotation of dynamism that is associated with the dance metaphor is picked up in the first of two Latin words used to translate *perichoresis*, namely *circumincessio*. It refers to a continual movement of the persons into the life of the others. The other Latin word that is used is *circumsessio*.[24] It also indicates mutual indwelling, but it conveys the sense of indwelling as a completed act. In and through the act of coinherence, there is complete satiation of the need for love; the divine persons rest in each other.

Jürgen Moltmann observes that the fact of this coinherence means that the Three live together in perfect harmony. They draw close to each other in the intimacy of perfect love, but at the same time they provide each other with space to be. 'The divine persons', he says, 'are "habitable" for one another, giving one another open life-space for their mutual indwelling. Each person is indwelling and room-giving at the same time.'[25] I suggest that this dynamic of intimate communion in which there is also open space provides the ideal for Christian community. We need to draw close to each other; our sharing of life together should be deep, intimate. At the same time, we need to give each other the space to be.

For most congregations, it is the closeness factor in the equation that is problematic. We are happy to give each other space – more than happy. Valuing our autonomy and personal freedom very highly, we do not want anyone trespassing on our personal space. A personal experience offers a good example of this fact. My family and I joined our current community of faith just over six months ago. Recently I preached a sermon on the theme of freedom in Christ. In the address I referred to the various personal 'hang-ups' that bind us. I listed a number of the more common ones, and then commented, 'I don't know if any of these belong to you; I don't know you well enough yet.' I should say at this point that in this particular congregation some people feel free to offer occasional quick comments and quips in response to something the preacher has said. This was one of those occasions. Obviously feeling a little uncomfortable about the thought that I might get close enough to pick up on some of his personal struggles, a listener interjected saying, 'Yeah, and you're not going to either!'

Our 'fellowship' together sometimes falls into what might be called pseudo-community. We point to all the communal activities that we share in together, and we tell ourselves that we are a close-knit fellowship. Certainly there is a degree of closeness, but we monitor our level of intimacy very carefully. It is kept within comfortable limits.

Let me offer another personal experience. In one parish in which I was the minister, I attended two cell groups. One met on a Wednesday night, the other on a Thursday afternoon. At each of the groups we did virtually the same thing. We prayed together and we reflected on a scripture passage. The aim in both groups was to relate the message of the text to our everyday lives. I always looked forward to the Thursday group. Our conversations together seemed to me to be important ones. I came away feeling uplifted and encouraged. The Wednesday night group, on the other hand, was a real struggle for me. I found that, try as I might, I simply could not get interested in it. It took me a little while to catch on to why I felt that way. The people, after all, were all very strong in their faith, they clearly cared about each other, and they entered into the discussions on the biblical texts with enthusiasm. Something very important, however, was missing. There seemed to be an unwritten rule that virtually everyone subscribed to: 'Never reveal the truth about yourself.' In response to questions concerning the text, the answers that were given were the 'correct' ones. That is, they were the responses that a 'good Christian' would be expected to make. No one in the group had any failings. No one had any doubts about their faith. No one had any problems – at least not any serious ones – that they needed to talk about. To be sure, there was always a very warm feeling in the group. There was laughter and good cheer. Often members would comment on how close they felt to each other. This was a very comfortable closeness, though. People kept each other at a safe distance. We talked a great deal about the meaning of a faithful Christian life, and all the while almost no one was prepared to tell the truth about him- or herself.

The members of the group thought of themselves as good friends. In some ways they were. They certainly enjoyed each other's company; they cared about each other; and they expressed their care in practical acts of kindness. Sadly, though, they didn't really know each other. In what follows, I want to develop a deeper understanding of Christian friendship. The perichoretic practice of intimacy-with-space will shape the discussion.

It is interesting to observe that the earliest Christians understood their communal life as an expression of friendship. At first glance, this may not seem to be the case. The Greek noun *philia* ('friendship') is used only once in the New Testament. Luke Timothy Johnson, however, points out that when the expressions that are used by the New Testament writers are set in the context of the prevailing Greco-Roman cultural milieu, the theme of friendship emerges quite clearly.[26] In the thought of the Greek and Roman philosophers, the idea that friends form one soul was of central importance. Commenting on the Jerusalem Church that is described in Acts, Johnson has this to say: 'By saying that the believers were "one soul," held "all things in common" and called nothing "their own," Luke described them as friends.'[27]

Johnson finds the same tonality of friendship in Paul's references to the community at Philippi. The *syn*-prefix is used frequently here. It means 'with' or 'together'. The prefix is used by Paul in conjunction with verbs such as 'struggle', 'rejoice', 'be formed', 'receive' and 'share'. These are the actions that define the group's life in Christ, and they are actions that are undertaken together. Paul also attaches the prefix to nouns such as 'sharer', 'soul', 'worker', 'soldier' and 'imitator'. In this way, the Christians at Philippi are seen to be yoked together. They are 'fellow-sharers', 'fellow-workers' and 'fellow-imitators'. 'If friendship in the Greek world is proverbially 'life together' (*symbios*)', writes Johnson, 'Paul could hardly find a more effective way to communicate to the Philippians that they were to be a community of friends.'[28]

When Augustine discusses life together in Christ, we find the same emphasis on close sharing. The grace of Christ draws believers together in a bond of friendship. Those who belong to the Body of Christ experience the highest possible form of unity. In a letter Augustine wrote to his friend, the future Pope Sixtus, he refers to Romans 5:5: 'The love of God has been poured out in our hearts through the Holy Spirit who has been given to us.' This great love has the power to bind the two friends together even though they are separated by distance: 'Whether absent or present in body, we wish to have you in one spirit by means of which love is poured in our hearts, so that wherever we may be in the flesh, our souls will be inseparable in every way.'[29] For Augustine, the Church is the place where we can expect to experience communion in its fullest expression. Paul Wadell captures this well when he writes: 'Given [Augustine's] belief that the most authentic, satisfying, and lasting intimacy comes from the union we have with one another in Christ, it would seem that the Church – the intimate friends of God – should be the community we need to learn and experience an intimacy that does not deceive.'[30]

Aelred of Rievaulx, a twelfth-century English Cistercian monk, also develops this theme of life in Christ as the ultimate expression of intimacy and friendship. Friendship in the community of faith, Aelred tells us, has its origin in Christ, is sustained by Christ and reaches its *telos* in Christ.[31] A perfect spiritual friendship, one that is grounded in the Lord, is one in which two persons unite as one spirit and the 'two form one'.[32] This union in love is expressed through bearing one another's burdens gladly, trusting each other implicitly and having the confidence to correct each other when necessary.

The ultimate aim of Christian friendship for Aelred is to grow into unity with Christ. In becoming one in heart and soul with our friends, we are made one spirit with Christ: 'Friend cleaving to friend in the Spirit of Christ is made with Christ but one heart and one soul, and so mounting aloft through degrees of love to friendship with Christ, he is made one spirit with him in one kiss.'[33]

We have seen that *perichoresis* involves both closeness and open space. What has emerged, though, in this brief survey of approaches to friendship and community from the New Testament era through to the Middle Ages is that the writers place a very strong emphasis on the element of closeness. In the modern period, the balance tends to be tipped towards the distance end. That is, while contemporary writers do highlight the importance of intimacy, they particularly stress the importance of respecting the autonomy and the right to self-determination of the other. While in the first fifteen hundred years of Christian history the idea of a spiritual union in friendship was accepted without question, Simone Weil goes so far as to say that two beings forming one is 'an adulterous union'.[34] Distance must be maintained and respected if there is to be a genuine friendship. Paul Goodliff makes the same point in this reflection on friendship in Christian community: 'In friendship we are aware that there is space to be ourselves, in the same way that in creation we are aware that God gives us space to be.'[35]

That the classic writers on spiritual friendship should emphasize unity of spirit is entirely understandable. Their thinking was strongly influenced by the ideas that were commonly promoted in the Greco-Roman world. In Plato and Aristotle, and in Cicero and Seneca, the same notions concerning friendship appear regularly.[36] Friends are one soul. The friend is another self. Friends live in harmony and are of one mind. Friendship is fellowship (*philia koinonia*) and 'life together' (*symbios*). Cicero's classic definition in his *de amicitia* draws all these elements together in a succinct fashion: 'Friendship is nothing else than an accord in all things, human and divine, conjoined with mutual goodwill and affection' (6.20).

In suggesting that we should take a lead from the ancients in their understanding and practice of spiritual friendship, I do not mean to gloss over the cultural differences separating us. Intimate sharing of life meant for them two people leading each other more deeply into Christ, the source of the unity between the friends. This involved praying together, challenging each other and bearing each other's burdens. While we share in this understanding of closeness in Christ, intimacy for us may also have a psychological or therapeutic dimension. That is, we may seek catharsis through talking about the deep feelings associated with the struggles, conflicts and ambiguities in our lives. This therapeutic aspect of spiritual friendship was not a feature of the experience of the ancients.

The point I want to make is simply that the ancient writers challenge us with the importance of closeness and unity in spiritual friendship. It presents as a timely message. Contemporary writers on friendship, for their part, are clearly influenced by the modern valuation of autonomy, freedom and individuality. We moderns prize our personal space and we tend to be fearful that others will trespass on it. The notion of becoming one with others in the Christian community is not immediately attractive to many. Our instinct is to maintain a healthy distance between self and others. Many of the fellowship activities in congregations are designed to support this desire for space. They allow us to move close enough to socialize, but not so close that we are threatened with intimacy.

One prominent development in church life, the small group movement, is driven to a large extent by a desire to move past the boundaries set up by traditional fellowship activities. The aim is to move beyond pseudo-community into a genuine sharing of life. Many groups do in fact achieve this goal. The members are prepared to commit themselves fully to each other. They take off their social masks and tell the truth about themselves. They open themselves to each other's pain and confusion and really listen. And they are ready to face the challenges of the gospel together. Others, however, fail in this task of growing together in faith and love. Robert Wuthnow identifies the failings incisively:

> Some small groups merely provide occasions for individuals to focus on themselves in the presence of others. The social contract binding them together asserts only the weakest of obligations. Come if you have time. Talk if you feel like it. Respect everyone's opinion. Never criticize. Leave quietly if you become dissatisfied.[37]

There is a genuine need to respect the personhood of the other. Others do need space to be. What Wuthnow describes is what might be called a counterfeit form of interpersonal distance. It indicates a view that others in the group have no right to make any significant claim on my time or my personhood. A commitment to the importance of maintaining distance in personal relationships does not mean that the other is allowed to make only the most gentle and innocuous of requests. There are claims that members may appropriately make on each other. Indeed, there can be no spiritual friendship unless they do make these claims. The key principle developed by the writers we have surveyed is that Christians need to make a genuine commitment to help each other grow in faith, hope and love. What this means is that the members of a group must open themselves to Christ and to each other.

I suggest that in practice this involves a commitment to openness and honesty. Truth-telling opens the way to a deeper relationship with God and with each other. It is important to be real concerning one's pain and struggle. A sanitized presentation of personal experience keeps real life at arm's length. It is a safe way to exist, but it diminishes and constrains the project of living authentically.

Another essential requirement for building an authentic communal life, I think, is a commitment to launching out into the deep waters. The Christian communal life that I have experienced has too often been oh so sensible, so restrained and so controlled. I have probably contributed to this culture more than I would like to admit. It is, after all, easier to fit in with a comfortable group mood than to challenge it. I have also been a part of small groups that have been vital and life-giving. These have been marked by courage and a readiness for risk.

Spiritual friendship cannot flourish in the absence of a commitment to intimacy. It is oppressive, however, unless it also respects the need for distance. Giving the other space to be requires a rejection of both the desire to dominate and the desire to please.[38] Both these tendencies are rooted in a need to close up the space between individuals. They are both driven by the same dynamic, namely, a push towards a unity of wills. Each tendency has its own particular way of expressing this dynamic, however. The person who wants to dominate is driven by a need to exert power over others. She needs the other to conform to her will in order to maintain control. The person who has an overweening desire to please, on the other hand, is afraid of being out of tune with the will of the other. When there is this failure in attunement, the result will likely be disapproval. She cannot bear the other person not being happy with her. In order to maintain a respectful distance, both the desire to dominate and the desire to please must disappear.

The importance of the concept of *perichoresis* for community and Christian friendship lies in the fact that it reminds us that unity and open space are equally important. It is only through opening ourselves to grace that we can hope to get near to balancing closeness and distance in our communal life. Simone Weil expresses this perfectly: 'Pure friendship is an image of that original and perfect friendship which belongs to the Trinity and which is the very essence of God. It is impossible for two human beings to be one while scrupulously respecting the distance which separates them, unless God is present in each of them.'[39]

Summary

In order to develop an understanding of what is required to build Christian community we have drawn upon the concepts of kenotic love and perichoretic relationality. Kenotic love involves making a space for the other. Unless we can empty ourselves of self-concern and self-interest we cannot be receptive to the joy and the pain, the disappointments and the hopes, of others. Being filled with self can also close us off to grace. It is only through God's action that we are able to open ourselves to other people.

The trinitarian dynamic of *perichoresis* involves both absolute intimacy and closeness on the one hand, and an open space on the other. It reminds us that claims to spiritual friendship are counterfeit unless there is an intimate sharing of life. It is only when people are prepared to draw close enough to face the truth – the truth about themselves and about God – that communion is established. Attending to *perichoresis* also highlights the importance of maintaining a respectful distance in the Christian community. In order to pay due regard to individuality and personal autonomy, others must be offered an open space in which to live.

The importance of worship in helping people to grow into kenotic love and a perichoretic style of relating has also been emphasized. The liturgy and worship of the Church offers a significant opportunity for Christians to learn the grammar of relationship. Small group life provides an important avenue for putting this learning into practice. The way in which pastoral leaders develop these core communal activities is of critical import.

Notes

1   Cf. D. Cunningham, 'Participation as a Trinitarian Virtue', *Toronto Journal of Theology* 14:1 (1998), pp. 7–25 (p. 13); P. Goodliff, *Care in a Confused Climate* (London: Darton, Longman and Todd, 1998), p. 141.
2   See J.B. Lounibos, 'Self-Emptying in Christian and Buddhist Spirituality', *Journal of Pastoral Counseling* 35 (2000), pp. 49–66 (p. 52).
3   See H.U. von Balthasar, *The Glory of the Lord*, vol. 7: *Theology: The New Covenant* (Edinburgh: T. & T. Clark, 1989), pp. 207–28.
4   Ibid., p. 217.
5   Ibid., p. 209.
6   Ibid., p. 214.
7   See J. Moltmann, *The Trinity and the Kingdom of God* (London: SCM Press, 1981), pp. 108–14.
8   Ibid., p. 111.
9   Ibid., p. 116ff.
10 See R. Gaillardetz, 'In Service of Communion', *Worship* 67 (1993), pp. 418–33 (p. 423).
11 See S. Post, 'The Inadequacy of Selflessness', *Journal of the American Academy of Religion* 56:2 (1989), pp. 213–23.
12 G. Wainwright, *Doxology: The Praise of God in Worship, Doctrine and Life* (New York: Oxford University Press, 1980), p. 23; cited in R. Leupp, *Knowing the Name of God: A Trinitarian Tapestry of Grace, Faith and Community* (Downers Grove, Ill.: InterVarsity Press, 1996), p. 160.
13 For a description of kenotic love in the Focalare movement, see D.W. Mitchell, 'Re-Creating Christian Community: A Response to Rita M. Gross', *Buddhist-Christian Studies* 23 (2003), pp. 21–32.
14 S. Weil, *Waiting on God* (London: Routledge and Kegan Paul, 1951), pp. 88–9.
15 See Leupp, *Knowing the Name*, p. 158.
16 Ibid.
17 Hadewijch, *The Complete Works* (New York: Paulist Press, 1980), pp. 99–100; cited in Leupp, *Knowing the Name*, pp. 154–5.
18 E.B. Anderson, 'A Constructive Task in Religious Education: Making Christian Selves', *Religious Education* 93:2 (1998), pp. 173–88 (p. 188).
19 See ibid., p. 188. See also P. Wadell, *Becoming Friends: Worship, Justice, and the Practice of Christian Friendship* (Grand Rapids, Mich.: Brazos Press, 2002), p. 22.
20 Cunningham, 'Participation', p. 8.
21 C.M. LaCugna, *God for Us* (HarperSanFrancisco, 1991), p. 271.
22 Cunningham, 'Participation', p. 19.
23 T.J. Scirghi, 'The Trinity: A Model for Belonging in Contemporary Society', *Ecumenical Review* 54:3 (2002), pp. 333–42 (p. 334).
24 For descriptions of *circumincessio* and *circumsessio* see Leupp, *Knowing the Name*, pp. 161–2, and J. Moltmann, 'Perichoresis: An Old Magic Word for a New Trinitarian Theology', in M.D. Meeks (ed.), *Trinity, Power and Community* (Nashville, Tenn.: Kingswood Books, 2000), p. 114.
25 Moltmann, 'Perichoresis', p. 114.

26 See L.T. Johnson, 'Making Connections: The Material Expression of Fellowship in the New Testament', *Interpretation* 58:2 (2004), pp. 158–71.
27 Ibid., p. 161.
28 Ibid., p. 163.
29 Augustine, *De Trinitate*, 9.4.6; cited in C. White, *Christian Friendship in the Fourth Century* (Cambridge University Press, 1992), p. 210.
30 Wadell, *Becoming Friends*, pp. 91–2.
31 See Aelred, *Spiritual Friendship*, 1:9.
32 Ibid., 2:11.
33 Ibid., 2:21.
34 Weil, *Waiting on God*, p. 136.
35 Goodliff, *Care in a Confused Climate*, p. 152.
36 For a brief survey of the Greco-Roman philosophical approaches to friendship, see Johnson, 'Making Connections', p. 160.
37 R. Wuthnow, 'Small Groups Forge New Notions of Community and the Sacred', *Christian Century* 110:35 (8 Dec. 1993), pp. 1236–40 (p. 1237).
38 See Weil, *Waiting on God*, p. 135.
39 Ibid., p. 137.

PART II
TRINITY AND PASTORAL COUNSELLING

PARTICIPATION IN LOVE

Chapter 5

Building the Counselling Alliance

The theme that will be developed in the second half of this book is *participation in love*. This defining trinitarian dynamic will be used to cast fresh light on three core counselling concerns: the therapeutic alliance, empathy and mirroring.

We make a start here by attending to the way in which the partners in the counselling project work together. I want to suggest that a 'three-dimensional' working alliance involving the counsellor, the counsellee and his or her support person(s) mirrors the loving participation that is the life of the Trinity. We have already seen that the idea that in human life we find a reflection, an imprint or a trace of the triune God was first advanced by Augustine (Chapter 1). He found in human love, for instance, a reflection of divine love. Thus, the three entities of the lover, the beloved and the love they share are said to mirror Father, Son and Holy Spirit. More recently, theologians have suggested that when relationships in the family[1] and in the Christian community[2] are at their best we find a mark of the triune life. It will be noted that the emphasis here is on the immanent rather than on the economic Trinity. That is, it is not what the divine persons do for us that is central in this theological approach, but rather the way in which the inner relational life of the Trinity exists as a model for human relations. Accordingly, the major concern in this chapter is to show how the loving relationality that is the triune God offers the ideal pattern for a counselling alliance.

The work of the French philosopher Francis Jacques on interpersonal life will play an important role in our discussion. I shall have much more to say about his thought below but will briefly introduce it here. Jacques contends that a communication event involves three agencies: the *I*, the *you* and *he/she*.[3] That is to say, in personal discourse two subjects address each other (the *I* and the *you*), but always in the context of an absent third party (the *he/she*). Here Jacques differs from the dialogical approach developed by Martin Buber and others. Buber believed that personhood is constituted through the meeting between the *I* and the *Thou*. While Buber argued for a dialogical understanding of human communication, Jacques contends that we must take a tri-agential approach.

A number of counsellors and therapists are inspired by Buber and construe their work in dialogical terms.[4] In this approach, the counselling process is interpreted as an *I–Thou* encounter. I want to follow those, however, who think of counselling in a tripersonal framework. Counsellors and therapists from a variety of schools are aware of the value of a support person(s) in effecting change. However, it is in the narrative approach that the tripersonal approach features most strongly. As a central part of their action plan, narrative counsellors sponsor a search for what I will call a 'nurturing third' (they refer to a member of an audience or of a team) who is able to support the re-authoring of the client's personal story. In the narrative approach, three parties play a role in the re-storying process: the counsellor, the counsellee, and the nurturing third. I find in this structure an image or mark of the triune God.

Underlying the approach developed in this essay is the conviction that relationality is at the heart of therapeutic work. A central issue, of course, is the precise nature of the relationality in the counselling alliance. In addressing this issue, I will refer to the tenderness (to use Brian Thorne's term) and the love-in-relationship that is strengthened by the power of the Spirit. The first task, however, is to describe Jacques's tri-agential approach to human communication.

A Tri-agential View of Personhood

In searching for a foundational characteristic of human existence, dialogical philosophers turn to language. Language is the primary way in which we communicate. Communication involves the creation of shared meaning with the other. John Macmurray observes that communication is therefore a personal act – one in which the *I* meets the *You*.[5] It is here that personhood is established. He wants to argue that 'the self is constituted by its relation to the Other; that it has its being in its relationship; and that this relationship is necessarily personal'.[6] Here Macmurray echoes the personalist perspective of Martin Buber.

In the utilitarian ethos of the modern society, life with others is construed in terms of a subject–object split. The other is viewed as an object, a thing, to be used and manipulated. Buber, however, imagines a new way of speaking in an attempt to reshape modern consciousness.[7] In place of the language of atomization – I, You, It, She, He – he offers the word-pairs *I–You* (or *I–Thou*) and *I–It*. A word-pair is immediately suggestive of communion. The one who speaks the word 'You' appears as a *person*, a person-in-relation. She is aware of her subjectivity, but she does not think of herself as a subject over against an object. Only egos construct themselves in terms of the over-against.

Francis Jacques, like Macmurray and Buber, identifies linguistic communication as fundamental in interpreting personhood. Self-realization is a process in which a person is continually defining him- or herself as an agent of communication. Personhood is actualized in the event that I am able to recognize myself through being able to receive an address from someone who calls me *you*. It is only when I respond to the one who says *you* that I am able to call myself *I*. The 'mystery of the self in two persons'[8] is an expression of the overlap of the two agencies, *I* and *you*. But this understanding of the linguistic event does not go far enough. We need also to refer to a third agency, the *he/she*. Interlocution, the reciprocity of address and response, cannot in and of itself establish the personhood of *I* and the *you*. Here Jacques observes that he is extending beyond Buber's interpretation of intersubjectivity through the key term of the *I–You*.[9] For Buber, as we have seen, a person becomes an *I* only through contact with a *you*. The love shared with the other constitutes the first person. But for Jacques, a person only becomes someone, an *I*, in a linguistic event in which three agencies – the *I*, the *you* and the *he/she* – participate: 'The third person is in a way relative to the first two, figuring as a third entity in relation to the circuit of their exchange. The value *he/she* is indeed separated from the *I* and *you* values of the participants, but it nevertheless remains in a certain relation to them.'[10]

This third party that forms the background to all communication is not, as Buber would have it, an *it*. Though he or she is spoken about, he or she is also a potential partner in an intersubjective exchange. If the *he/she* represented a person cut out of all communication the third party would exist as a non-person. But the *he/she* about whom I am speaking to you has the potential to engage in communication. He or she 'is virtually addressable by you and by me'.[11] It is possible, for example, to contact him or her by telephone. It is also important to realize that the *he/she* is not an optional extra. Jacques is not saying that an absent third party is only *sometimes* a factor in interpersonal discourse. Rather, his point is that even when there is no explicit reference to a third, the *he/she* must be there to make the communication meaningful.

When Jacques says that the third party is a necessary element in every communication event he implies that he or she is there either *explicitly* or *tacitly*. Bill and Mary are engaged in conversation. In the course of their chat, Mary is talking about her good friend, Jenny. The communication event is constituted by an *I* (Mary), a *you* (Bill), and a *she* (Jenny). In this case, Jenny functions as an *explicit* third entity.

Now let us imagine that Bill and Mary are both very keen photographers and that in a later conversation they are talking about their current projects. Bill is discussing in great detail how he is using a lens he has just acquired to create a particular effect. It might seem on the surface that there is no absent third party to be found in this discussion. It is a conversation between two people about photographic techniques. And yet, the conversation is only possible because of an absent *he/she*. Someone taught Bill about photography (either in person or through something she or he had written). That person functions tacitly in the conversation as a third party. Bill is not thinking about her or him at this particular moment. Nevertheless, the photographer teacher is a participant in the communication event.

Now of course there may have been a number of people who have helped Bill in his development as a photographer. They all participate tacitly in the conversation between Bill and Mary. Similarly, in the course of their previous conversation in which Jenny featured, Bill and Mary might also have referred to a number of their other friends. Jacques's *he/she* is to be understood as symbolically representing the absent others that play a constitutive role in a communication event. In a similar way, when I refer to the nurturing third in the counselling alliance, I am using a representative symbol. There may be a number of support persons that the counsellor and the counsellee enlist together. Indeed, the aim is to find as many as possible.

Communication, then, has a tripersonal structure. Personhood is constituted through a tripersonal system of interacting agencies. What is particularly interesting for our present discussion is that Jacques sees this 'trinitariness' as a 'beautiful mirror' of the divine Trinity. He refers to the Trinity in terms of what I would call Being-in-Relation:

> The Trinity founds within the divine Being itself nothing less than the relation by which persons are constituted. Metaphorically, how can this be? I shall go so far as to say that

God Himself *is* relationally. God is He who is, the One who makes relations possible, because He Himself is a relation.[12]

This God who *is* relationally is 'the archetype … of a tripersonal humanity',[13] and so we are led to the hypothesis that 'the human person is basically relational on the level of absolute being and absolute value'.[14]

There are two ideas at the centre of Jacques's approach that have also been very important for us. First, in his suggestion that the tripersonal nature of the communication event mirrors the Trinity, Jacques engages with the *vestigia trinitatis* tradition. To use David Cunningham's language, the interpersonal triad constitutes a mark of the triune God. The second idea is that relationality is the core concept when it comes to interpreting triune life. Cunningham brings both of these ideas together in identifying the perichoretic traces in human relations. To give just one example from his work, he observes that relations in the family (at least in the ideal case) should be marked by communion and participation. Referring to his own experience, he says: 'I am "related" to my wife and my daughters, yes, but more than this: I dwell in their lives and they in mine. They are fundamentally constitutive of who "I" am.'[15]

The Tripersonal Shape of the Counselling Alliance

In looking at the way in which Francis Jacques finds a tri-agential structure underlying the constitution of the person, we have seen that any communication event involves not only the *I* and the *you* but also an absent third party, a *he/she*. What, we need to ask, does this have to say in the context of the counselling relationship? Counsellors and therapists from a variety of schools of thought are aware of the importance of resource persons who can support the client. It is in the narrative school, however, that the role of the third party is most fully developed. Narrative counsellors include as part of their methodology a search for what might be called a 'nurturing third'. This support person acts to strengthen the emerging counter-story.

The two key underlying and related premises of narrative counselling are that human existence has a storied structure and that all social reality is a human construct. That there is a narrative structure in personal and communal life is a widely held view. There is ample evidence that humans generate stories to make sense of their lives. Narrative therapists use this idea as a foundational stone for their theory and practice. People, they observe, make meaning through the stories they tell about themselves.[16] The way in which meaning is made, however, is shaped by the prevailing cultural myths.[17] It follows, say the narrative counsellors, that problem-bound stories are set in dominant cultural stories and this fact needs to be exposed through deconstructive analysis. Certain ideas, beliefs and values embedded in the social and cultural milieu contribute to the problem. When these are laid bare the client has the possibility of challenging them.

An important activity in the narrative approach is the discovery of what Michael White calls 'unique outcomes' (borrowed from Erving Goffman) or 'sparkling moments'.[18] These are attitudes or actions that are exceptions to the rules of the problem. For example, a person who is usually very timid asserts herself in a relationship. Or a person suffering from anxiety experiences times of relative peace and calm. It is almost always the case, though, that these exceptional moments are lost in the thickness of the problem-saturated story. The role of the narrative counsellor here is twofold. First, she must help the client assemble as many unique outcomes as possible.[19] If only one or two come to light, the client may feel that these are meaningless aberrations. Monk suggests that the process is akin to gathering sticks in building up a fire. 'The twigs and sticks referred to here are the person's positive lived moments. It is my task as counsellor to identify these favored moments and bring them to the awareness of the client. The art in this approach is knowing where to look and recognizing the unstoried moment when you see it.'[20]

The second task of the narrative counsellor in relation to unique outcomes is helping the client make these moments vivid and strong. Narrative counsellors are very thorough and persistent in this regard. They seek to assist the client in recalling as much detail as possible about the people, places, feelings and thoughts associated with the sparkling moment. The unique outcomes form the material out of which the counterplot will be storied. The problem-saturated story is powerful and authoritative; the alternative story needs to be robust enough to supplant it as a primary determinant of the client's experience of life. In assembling as many sparkling moments as possible, and in assisting the client to thicken the description of these moments, the plot material for a strong counter-story becomes available.

Recognizing how difficult it is to develop an alternative story, narrative counsellors intentionally seek out friends and family members who will be able to support this development. 'An *appreciative audience* to new developments is deliberately sought out. For most of us, it is not possible to make radical changes in our lives without somebody cheering us on.'[21] The question that is most commonly employed in helping the client identify a support person or persons is along the lines, 'Who would be least surprised to hear that you did this or thought that?'[22] Freedman and Combs suggest other useful questions:

Who would be most interested to learn of this step you've taken? Why would that interest her so? How could you let her know?

Who in your current life would have predicted that you would make this kind of commitment? What do they know about you that would have led them to make this prediction? How would knowing about this step support this knowledge about you? Would that be helpful to you? How? How would you let them know?

Who would most appreciate this event we've been talking about? What might he learn about you if you let him in on it that would be of interest to him? What might he say to you about this? How could you initiate such a conversation?[23]

There is, then, a conviction that there is a community of support available to the client, and that this community has a vital role to play in healing and growth. To use some of the terms we developed earlier in our discussion of Jacques's approach, behind or under the communication of the client to the counsellor – that is, on a tacit level – there are third parties who have a crucial function. That function involves affirmation, support and strengthening. The skill the counsellor needs is the framing of the questions that will allow the client to move her relationship to the nurturing third from a tacit to an explicit level.

There is in narrative counselling, however, a step beyond this shifting of the encouraging third party from tacit to explicit awareness. Counsellors work with the assumption that the client might actually engage the third in a conversation. In reflecting together on the sparkling moments, the significance of these moments is understood more fully and they become even more real and powerful. Freedman and Combs suggest that even when no such conversation takes place, there is still a very real benefit. The supportive third person develops in the imagination of the client, and an 'imaginary conversation'[24] may make a significant contribution.

Even when it is no longer possible to make contact with the nurturing third – because she or he is dead – her or his influence can be strong. Winslade and Monk illustrate this through recounting the case of Elaine, a 13-year-old diagnosed with clinical depression who had been receiving medication for several weeks before coming for counselling.[25] The counsellor asked Elaine how she kept going without being totally swamped by the depression. Elaine responded by saying that she would think of her grandfather's indomitable spirit. It was his inner strength and sense of hope that sustained him when Elaine's grandmother died. Sensing the potential empowerment the grandfather could provide, the counsellor asked: 'Would your grandad be surprised to hear the conversation we are having now about how you are beginning to drive depression out of your life?' This line of inquiry 'led Elaine to redescribe herself as symbolically carrying forward her grandfather's spirit. She felt less alone in her struggle against depression'.[26]

This need for a nurturing third is so urgent that sometimes it is not even necessary to ask the question that would elicit him or her. In my experience, some counsellees will spontaneously call on the support of their 'cheer squad'. David came to see me because of what he experienced as persecution from his boss, the principal of the school in which he was working. Over a period of time, David received numerous e-mails criticizing some element of his work. When a parent raised a concern about David's discipline of her daughter, the principal immediately took her side and proceeded to berate him. After thirty years in the teaching vocation, David was experiencing for the first time a significant failure in professional self-confidence. The end result of these experiences was clinical depression.

When David first came to see me, he believed that he would have to stick out the job. He was convinced that getting another one at his age would be almost impossible. During the course of the counselling, however, this view proved to be overly pessimistic; he received a job offer and decided to accept it. David continued our sessions in order to process what he had been suffering through and to attempt to regain his confidence.

As I listened, I heard two sets of stories. The first set of stories was, of course, about the unjust and soul-destroying way his principal was treating him. David knew on one level that he was a very able teacher, but this crushing experience resulted in self-doubt. I didn't have to ask him the question, 'Who knows you as an excellent teacher and as a fine person?' David spontaneously told a series of stories from his teaching past. There were stories about young teachers he had mentored. I heard about their deep appreciation of his belief in them and his help with their careers. I listened to stories about innovative teaching programmes and the way students warmly received them. In our conversations the nurturing third was often present. He or she did not need my bidding in order to come to David's aid. David instinctively knew that he needed a cheer squad to help him rebuild his confidence. My role was one of enhancing the power of the stories through positive mirroring. As I reflected back the highlights in these stories and pondered on their significance, they became an even stronger resource for David in countering the story of incompetence and failure sponsored by his principal.

These three – the counsellor, the counsellee and the nurturing third – share together in the development of a counter-story. In this relational alliance there is an echo of the Trinity. Of course, it is a faint echo. There are clearly significant differences between the relational life of the triune God and that of humans. The most obvious is that nowhere in human existence do we find three personal relations within the one entity. I contend, though, that wherever we find persons connected to each other in a communion of love it is appropriate to speak of a mark of the Trinity.

Tender Love, Trinity and the Counselling Alliance

I have been arguing that the optimal counselling alliance is one in which counsellor, counsellee and the nurturing third party all participate fully. I want now to ask the question, What are the personal qualities that these three manifest when they maximally participate in the work of healing and growth? I want to focus primarily on the counsellor and on the support person. The touchstones in counselling work are empathy, unconditional positive regard, and congruence. In a strong counselling alliance, both the counsellor and the nurturing third will be persons who are empathic, accepting and genuine. However, I want to suggest that they will also manifest another quality, namely, what the British psychotherapist Brian Thorne calls 'tenderness'.

While fully appreciating the value of, and power in, the three therapeutic touchstones, Thorne contends that there is yet another level of personal participation.[27] He cannot find the word that fully describes this experience; the closest he can get is 'tenderness'. 'Here is a word which means both vulnerable and warmly affectionate, easily crushed and merciful, not tough [but rather] sympathetic. It seems to incorporate both weakness and gentle strength, great fragility and great constancy.'[28] Struggling to capture this very real but at the same time quite elusive quality, Thorne strings together a number of descriptors.[29] This is a quality that 'irradiates the whole person'. It 'communicates through its responsive vulnerability that suffering and healing are interwoven'. Finally, the one who has this quality is able to 'move between the worlds of the physical, the emotional, the cognitive and the mystical without strain'. Thorne has no hesitation in saying that when he participates in the counselling relationship in this intense and profound way 'my client and I are caught up in a stream of love'.[30]

James Olthuis also refers to therapy as entering a stream of love.[31] The power in therapy is not so much in techniques and psychological knowledge, but rather in the love that fills the 'wild space' between therapist and client. The sphere of the between is wild because it is uncharted, unpredictable and risky. Those who enter it must be prepared to be vulnerable, to suffer with, and to offer profound respect and affirmation. In Thorne's language, they must be ready to give tender love. It is the Spirit of Christ that makes such love possible. 'In this process, love – the love of God – not reason, nor method creates a healing connection. Sharing this cosmic process in which the Spirit is afoot in the world heals our isolation, suffering-with leads to a celebrating-with, grace and blessing.'[32]

The extent to which the quality of tender love exists in the counselling alliance is, of course, only partially within the control of the counsellor. While through prayer, reflection on experience and openness to the Spirit a Christian counsellor can aim to grow in her capacity for tender love, she has no input into the personal qualities of the nurturing third party. This is someone nominated by the counsellee, and she or he may not even be still with us. I am simply making the point that a maximally effective counselling alliance will involve full participation from all three parties, and that from the side of the counsellor and the supportive third this maximal participation involves tender love. The counsellor can only hope that there is a support person available to the counsellee who has the valuable personal qualities we have been discussing. When this is the case, the counselling alliance will be much the richer for it.

When it comes to the counsellee, his full participation requires honesty, courage, vulnerability and perseverance. To engage fully he also needs the grace to receive the personal gifts offered by both the counsellor and the nurturing third party.

I want to suggest, further, that the full participation in the counselling alliance that I have been describing echoes the inner life of the Trinity. 'Participation' is also a key word in trinitarian theology. It is a mutual coinherence in love (*perichoresis*) that defines the life of the triune God. This life is not that of three centres of initiative that somehow come together in a loving relationship. The Trinity is a relationship of love without remainder. The God of love 'is *wholly constituted* by relationality'.[33] This mutual coinherence is what Cunningham calls 'the trinitarian virtue of participation'.[34] He suggests that when we dwell in others and they dwell in us our life together is marked by this virtue. The empathy, love and tenderness that are shared in the counselling alliance at its best echo the life of the Trinity.

Summary

Underlying all of our discussion of the counselling alliance is the conviction that relationship is its core. It is the relationship that heals. Some counsellors influenced by the dialogical philosophy of Martin Buber construe their engagement with the client in terms of an *I–You* relation. Following the lead of the narrative therapists, however, it was suggested that there is real value in broadening the framework of counselling work to include a *he/she*, the nurturing third. Francis Jacques sees in the triad of *I*, *you* and *he/she* that constitutes a communication event a 'beautiful mirror' of the Trinity. Taking our cue from Jacques, it has been argued that the tripersonal alliance in counselling is also an image of the triune life.

The question of the nature of the relationships in the counselling alliance was also addressed. A tender participation in the life of the other is at the heart of healing relationships. Tenderness is characterized by empathy, vulnerability, suffering with, deep respect and strong affirmation. We are able to love in this way when we are lit up by the love of the Spirit of Christ.

Notes

1   See D. Cunningham, *These Three Are One: The Practice of Trinitarian Theology* (Oxford: Blackwell, 1998).
2   See P. Fox, *God as Communion* (Collegeville, Minn.: Liturgical Press, 2001).
3   F. Jacques, *Difference and Subjectivity*, trans. A. Rothwell (New Haven, Conn.: Yale University Press, 1991).
4   See, for example, M. Friedman, 'Buber's Philosophy as the Basis for Dialogical Psychotherapy and Contextual Therapy', *Journal of Humanistic Psychology* 38 (1998), pp. 25–40; R. Hobson, *Forms of Feeling* (London: Tavistock Publications, 1985); R. Hycner, *Between Person and Person* (Highland, NY: Gestalt Journal, 1991).
5   J. Macmurray, *Persons in Relation* (London: Faber and Faber, 1961).
6   Ibid., p. 17.
7   See M. Buber, *I and You*, trans. W. Kaufmann (Edinburgh: T. & T. Clark, 1970) [first published 1919].
8   Jacques, *Difference and Subjectivity*, p. 31.
9   See ibid., p. 32.
10 Ibid., p. 34.
11 Ibid., p. 35.
12 Ibid., p. 69.
13 Ibid., p. 69.
14 Ibid., p. 69.
15 Cunningham, *These Three Are One*, p. 169.
16 See M. White and D. Epston, *Narrative Means to Therapeutic Ends* (Adelaide: Dulwich Centre Publications, 1990), p. 10.
17 This view is central in the narrative approach. See, for example, W. Drewery and J. Winslade, 'The Theoretical Story of Narrative Therapy', in G. Monk et al (eds), *Narrative Therapy in Practice* (San Francisco: Jossey-Bass, 1997), pp. 32–52; J. Freedman and G. Combs, *Narrative Therapy* (New York: W.W. Norton, 1996); A. Morgan, *What is Narrative Therapy?* (Adelaide: Dulwich Centre Publications, 2000).
18 White and Epston, *Narrative Means*, p. 15.
19 W. McKenzie and G. Monk, 'Learning and Teaching Narrative Ideas', in Monk et al (eds), *Narrative Therapy*, pp. 82–117 (p. 108).
20 G. Monk, 'How Narrative Therapy Works', ibid., pp. 3–31 (p. 17).
21 J. Winslade and G. Monk, *Narrative Counseling in Schools* (Thousand Oaks, Calif.: Sage Publications, 1999), p. 15.
22 See McKenzie and Monk, 'Learning and Teaching Narrative Ideas', p. 111; Monk, 'How Narrative Therapy Works', p. 21; Morgan, *What is Narrative Therapy?*, p. 69.
23 Freedman and Combs, *Narrative Therapy*, p. 238.
24 Ibid., p. 239.
25 See Winslade and Monk, *Narrative Counseling*, p. 33ff.
26 Ibid., p. 47.
27 See B. Thorne, *Person-Centred Counselling: Therapeutic and Spiritual Dimensions* (London: Whurr, 1991).

28   Ibid., p. 75.
29   See ibid., p. 76.
30   Ibid., p. 77.
31   See J. Olthuis, 'Being-with: Toward a Relational Psychotherapy', *Journal of Psychology
      and Christianity* 13 (1994), pp. 217–31; idem, 'Dancing Together in the Wild Spaces
      of Love: Postmodernism, Psychotherapy, and the Spirit of God', *Journal of Psychology
      and Christianity* 18 (1999), pp. 140–52.
32   Olthuis, 'Dancing Together', p. 150.
33   Cunningham, *These Three Are One*, p. 165.
34   Ibid.

Chapter 6

Empathy, Communion and Identity

In the latter part of the previous chapter, attention was drawn to the important role tender love plays in therapeutic work. Mention was made of the fact that empathy features in therapeutic tenderness. Here we will be attending to two key functions of empathy, namely its capacity to (1) heal the pain of aloneness, and (2) support identity consolidation.

To guide our trinitarian analysis of empathy, we will pick up on the way in which the Orthodox theologian John Zizioulas develops two central notions in trinitarian theology. The first is the formula of the Cappadocian theologians, according to which the Trinity is conceived as 'persons in communion'. It was through the use of the term *koinonia* that the Cappadocians aimed to maintain the unity within the triune God. The second key principle posited by Zizioulas is that the relations in the Trinity establish the identity of the divine persons. What it is to be Father, Son and Holy Spirit is fixed in and through the acts of begetting and spirating by the Father.

'Communion' and 'relationship' are terms that express the trinitarian virtue that we are concentrating on in this second half, *participation*.[1] The persons in the Trinity participate in each other's being. Participation points to a foundational activity in counselling, namely empathy. To empathize is to share in the experience of another. It involves 'transposing oneself into the thinking, feeling and acting of another'.[2] The participation in the triune God is full and complete. The persons know and understand each other perfectly. Counsellors strive to know and understand the experiences of their clients as fully as possible, but they encounter a limit in this striving. Hence, triune participation establishes an ideal for empathic participation.

In exploring the connections between triune and therapeutic participation, we will take our cues from the notions of communion and identity-through-relations that are central in Zizioulas's interpretation of the Trinity. The communion in the Trinity points to a vitally important function of empathy, namely, the overcoming of the experience of isolation and aloneness. An empathic connection with another says, 'You are not alone; I am with you in this.' We will see that, while in both the triune God and the empathic relation there is a sharing of life that creates communion, the manner of that sharing is fundamentally different. Communion in the Trinity is expressed on the level of ontology (through the being of the divine persons), whereas in an empathic relationship communion takes place on the level of imagination. With this in mind, the notion of 'imaginative projection', so important in an accurate understanding of empathy, will be discussed.

The trinitarian idea of identity-through-relations, secondly, will lead us into reflection on another key function of empathy. That key role is the knitting together of the various fragments of the self into a coherent sense of 'I'. Empathy involves more than simply reflecting back elements in an established sense of identity. It actually contributes to the process of identity formation in the client. More specifically, empathy both stimulates personal discovery in the client and creates new possibilities for her sense of self.

The process that we will engage in, then, is a dialogue between the trinitarian theology of Zizioulas and certain important writings on empathy. We begin with the Orthodox theologian's treatment of the Cappadocian formula and its key terms of 'person' and 'communion'.

Zizioulas and 'Persons in Communion'

The genius of the Cappadocian theologians (Basil the Great, Gregory of Nazianus, Gregory of Nyssa) was the way in which they maintained both the unity of God and the full and complete being of each of the persons through the formula 'persons in communion' (*hypostases en koinonia*). Through the use of *hypostasis* they ensured that each person was granted full being. The unity in the triune God was protected through the employment of *koinonia*.

In *Being as Communion*,[3] Zizioulas begins by showing how the linkage between *hypostasis* and the concept of person was achieved. This connection was, in fact, entirely foreign to an ancient Greek way of thinking, and so the Cappadocians here recorded quite an achievement. Zizioulas also wants to show how the early Greek theologians grounded the ontological principle of the life of God (the being of God) not in substance but in a person, in the Father. This is most significant because it takes us from the abstract (substance) into the dynamic life of relation. The Fatherhood of God is expressed through the relations of begetting the Son and bringing forth the Holy Spirit. God's being is grounded in relation, in the communion established between the three persons.

Zizioulas begins by observing that it was not possible in ancient Greek thought to create a true ontology of the person.[4] To find the reason for this it is necessary to focus on the early Greek valuation of unity and harmony. The ancient Greeks held to the principle that being ultimately constitutes a unity even though there is a multiplicity of existent entities. Concrete existent beings owe their being in the final analysis to the 'one' being. The unity of all that is is the ultimate principle of being, and all differentiation into separate beings is regarded as a fall from being. A cosmos of unity and harmony is the ideal. There is ultimately no place for absolute freedom, even in the human, because this would result in a tear in the harmony of the cosmos. Freedom results in unexpected events. Freedom breaks apart the unity of the world. It thereby sets itself at odds with reason (*logos*), whose role is to draw all things together.

Ancient Greek tragedy, Zizioulas points out, was the forum in which the human's place in the cosmos of harmony was worked out.[5] It is here that the term 'person' (*prosopon*) appears in ancient Greek usage. The term is connected with the mask used in the theatre. In the Greek tragedies, the conflict between human freedom and rational necessity is worked out. But why is there this link with the mask? 'As a result of this mask, man – the actor, but properly also the spectator – has acquired a certain taste of freedom, a certain specific "hypostasis", a certain identity, which the rational and moral harmony of the world in which he lives denies him.'[6] In the ancient Greek world, for someone to be a person means that she has something added to her being. The 'person' is an adjunct to a human being; it is not her true 'hypostasis'. 'Hypostasis' is not descriptive of personhood but rather of 'nature' or 'substance'.

The same state of affairs, notes Zizioulas, existed in early Roman thought.[7] *Persona* in its sociological and legal usage has the same theatrical nuance of a role. It refers to the role one plays in one's social and legal relationships. Roman thought is basically organizational and social. In this cognitive framework, men and women are construed not in ontological terms but in terms of their relationship to others. What is of primary importance is the way persons form associations, enter into contracts, and generally organize human life in a state. Personhood is again viewed as an adjunct to concrete ontological being. It is something that permits the person to express more than one *prosopon*, to play a number of different roles. Thus, both *prosopon* and *persona* function only as pointers to the person. Both terms serve to express the conviction that the personal dimension of human life is not identical with the essence of reality, with the true being of humanity.

Zizioulas points out that it is in the thought of the early Greek theologians that we first see an identification of 'person' with the being of the human.[8] This identification emerged in the process of grappling with the notion that God is Father, Son and Holy Spirit, but at the same time one God. The Greek theologians were unhappy with Tertullian's (a theologian of the West) formulation of *una substantia, tres personae* because the term 'person' did not for them have an ontological referent. That is, they did not believe that it was capable of expressing the full and complete being in the three. The formula, they were convinced, led towards Sabellianism with its notion of God manifesting in three 'roles'. In seeking to assign full being to each of the three, they identified *hypostasis* with person.

Over against the tendency of the theologians in the West to locate the ontological principle of God in the substance of God, the Greeks turned to the *hypostasis*. That is to say, they related the ontological dimension in God to the personhood in God. The Father is the cause of God's existence: 'God, as Father, and not as substance, perpetually confirms through "being" His *free* will to exist. And it is precisely His trinitarian existence that constitutes this confirmation: the Father out of love – that is, freely – begets the Son and brings forth the Spirit.'[9] In the Trinity, person implies communion. The Father shares his life with the Son and the Holy Spirit.

Having linked 'person' with *hypostasis* and thereby affirming its ontological status, the Cappadocian theologians had a suitable formula with which to refer to the Trinity, namely, *mia ousia – tries hypostaseis*. The divine substance (*ousia*) is shared by three persons. Further, the substance of God never exists by itself; it always exists through hypostasis, through a mode of existence.

Basil recognized that over against Sabellianism it was necessary to safeguard both the distinction between the persons and their ontological status (they have full being; they are not simply 'modes' of divine being). It was also essential to maintain the unity of the Godhead. He considered that the best way to hold together both the unity of God and the ontological integrity of the persons is through the use of *koinonia* (communion). 'Wherein in the communion of the substance we maintain that there is no mutual approach or intercommunion of those notes of indication perceived in the Trinity, whereby is set forth the proper peculiarity of the Persons delivered in the faith, each of these being distinctively apprehended by His own notes.'[10] In order to affirm the importance of *koinonia* in the life of the Trinity, Basil decided to use a doxology different from the conventional one of the early centuries, 'Glory be to the Father through (*dia*) the Son in (*en*) the Holy Spirit.'[11] He opted instead for 'Glory be to the Father with (*syn*) the Son, with (*syn*) the Holy Spirit'. In this way, he emphasized that the oneness of God is to be found in the *koinonia* of the three persons.

Through the formula 'persons in communion' the Cappadocian theologians made an important contribution. *Koinonia* provides a way of maintaining the unity of God, while associating *hypostasis* with person allows the maintenance of both the distinctiveness of the persons and their ontological integrity.

If communion is at the heart of the triune life, it is also vitally important in pastoral relationships. To be in communion with another is to share in her life. It involves dwelling in, and being indwelt by, that person. Those of us engaged in pastoral counselling will immediately begin to think of empathy when the language of 'dwelling in the other' is used.

Participation, Empathy and 'Imaginative Projection'

In taking into account the relational dimension in the life of God, David Cunningham (as we saw in the previous chapter) suggests that there is a trinitarian virtue called *participation*.[12] Participation in the triune life, he notes, has been traditionally expressed through the term *perichoresis*. It 'describes the Three as indwelling and interpenetrating one another so completely that we can never intelligibly speak of one without involving, at least implicitly, the other two as well. The Three exist in a dynamic interrelationship with one another, giving to and receiving from one another what they most properly are.'[13] Cunningham suggests that the virtue of participation can be developed in our lives too. He notes that the usual meaning of *participate* is 'to take part in'. So, for example, we take part in sports, in meetings, in worship. But of course he is not interested in participation in some*thing*, but rather in some*one*. 'For example, to "participate in the sufferings of another" is to make another's pain one's own – perhaps by subjecting oneself to similar treatment, or empathizing with another to the greatest possible degree.'[14] It is a natural connection to make: the trinitarian virtue of participation is especially prominent in empathy. In saying this, one must also say straight away that there are clearly a number of differences between triune participation and human empathy. To begin with, there is not the same mutuality in therapeutic empathy. The participation in the experience of the other comes almost exclusively from the side of the counsellor. Secondly, in the communion between the divine persons the knowledge and understanding of each other is absolute, complete and perfect. Here we have an ideal for therapeutic empathy. We strive to know and understand the experience of the other as fully as possible. But we know that we can never reach the ideal. Our understanding is never total. Quite apart from our own limitations, we must contend with the fact that the self-understanding of the other is not complete. The ideal is important, however. It leads us on towards the fullest understanding of the client that we are capable of.

Even the relatively limited participation that is possible on the human level, though, is powerful. Empathy establishes a communion that mitigates 'the metaphysical aloneness of the other'.[15]

There is another difference between divine and therapeutic participation. The communion between the triune persons is on the level of ontology. Empathic communion is established on the level of imagination. Indeed, *imagination* is a key term in an accurate description of the empathic process. Empathy is sometimes construed in terms of a focussing inwards in which one uses one's own feelings as a point of contact with what the other is experiencing. That is, if one senses despair in the other, one turns to one's own experiences to get in touch with that feeling. While there is some value in this exercise, it does not take us to the heart of what empathy is. Rather than a turning in to the self, empathy is essentially a projecting into the experience of the other through the imagination. In a word, it is an 'imaginative projection'.[16] As Alfred Margulies puts it, empathy is an 'active, searching quality of entering the other's world'.[17] This entering the other's world requires that one maintain the interpersonal boundary. Carl Rogers has this to say:

> To sense the client's private world as if it were your own, but without ever losing the 'as if' quality – this is empathy, and this seems essential to therapy. To sense the client's anger, fear, or confusion as if it were your own, yet without your own anger, fear, or confusion getting bound up with it, is the condition we are endeavoring to describe.[18]

The 'as if' quality in empathic projection is very important, I think. There is a need to maintain the boundary between oneself and the other. A real meeting between two people requires that both maintain their own individual identities. To forget that the other's anger, frustration and confusion are hers and not one's own introduces confusion into the relationship. This is something that Rogers consistently warned against. It is perhaps interesting to recall that it is also something that the Cappadocian theologians cautioned against in their trinitarian theology. There is fullness of communion in the life of the Godhead, but each person 'is distinctively apprehended by His own note'. Or as Cunningham puts it, there is particularity as well as participation.[19]

With this emphasis on boundaries in mind, it is puzzling to note that in a later (1980) definition of empathy Rogers shows himself to be much less concerned about the possibility of identification. To enter the private world of the client

> means that for the time being, you lay aside your own views and values … In some sense it means that you lay aside yourself; this can only be done by persons who are secure enough in themselves that they know they will not get lost in what may turn out to be the strange and bizarre world of the other, and that they can comfortably return to their own world when they wish.[20]

Why the change? Was it really the case that late in his life Rogers forgot about the warnings he had sounded throughout his career? Here I find the explanation offered by Ken Cissna and Rob Anderson helpful.[21] They make three points. First, the passage appears in a book in which Rogers uses a personal and informal style in order to reach a wide lay audience. Second, the passage appears in the same essay that contains his more rigorous 1959 definition. Third, the passage in question 'is highly metaphorical, imprecise and qualified'.[22] This is not a case of Rogers being inconsistent, they rightly point out, as much as of him being rhetorically attuned to his (non-scholarly) audience. We should take it that the importance of maintaining one's own personal ground in the empathic act was always in the forefront of Rogers's thinking.

In order 'to sense the client's private world as if it were your own' it is necessary to meet it on its own terms. Marie McCarthy puts it well:

> In empathic engagement I project myself into the object of contemplation in order to understand him or her. The projection involved here is not merely that of seeing my own preconceptions, of seeing what I expected to see. It is a projection in which I come to see what's really there 'by getting into it' ... In projecting myself into the other's world, I take that world seriously, on its own terms.[23]

This engagement with the inner world on its own terms requires from the empathizer the discipline of 'bracketing'. She 'brackets out' her own biases and preconceptions and thus gives herself the best chance to see experience as the client sees it. Of course, this is always an ideal. It is not in fact possible to set aside one's own values and perspectives completely. These will always intrude to some extent. The discipline of bracketing serves to minimize this intrusion.

Through imaginative projection, then, it is possible to participate in the experience of the other. The communion that is established in this act serves the vitally important role of mitigating her 'metaphysical aloneness'. There is, it needs to be noted, another key function performed by empathy. The empathic act helps a person pull together her fragmented subselves. As the subselves begin to knit together, a stronger sense of identity emerges.

Empathy and Identity-through-Relationship

Though there is no fragmentation in the divine persons, there is a parallel that exists between this function of empathy and the life of the Trinity. Zizioulas sees in the mutual participation of the Three the establishment of identity. Each person is who he (she) is through relationship. The otherness of each person (as Father, as Son, as Spirit) is determined in and through the relations they share in. The Father begets the Son, and breathes out the Spirit. (This, of course, contrasts with the Western theological tradition, according to which the Spirit proceeds from both the Father and the Son. The principle is the same in both traditions, however: identity is established through the relationality that is the triune God.) According to Zizioulas, particularity in the Trinity is constituted through the divine relations: 'This hypostatic fullness as otherness can emerge only through a relationship so constitutive ontologically that relating is not consequent upon being but is being itself.'[24] Since the relations are constituted in and through the being of the Three, the knowledge and understanding that is shared is perfect. Though this is not possible on the human level, there is nevertheless an analogy to be drawn. Zizioulas's point is that identity in the Godhead emerges through relationship.

Before attempting to show how identity is constituted through empathic attunement, I should define what is meant by the term 'personal identity'. In very general terms, it refers to continuity and integration in the self and in its projects. The philosopher Terence Cave defines the 'interior or subjective self' as 'a kind of elastic bag of idiosyncrasies, personal habits, private memories, private stories, or private fictions'.[25] (Importantly, he highlights the fact that narrative has the power to determine sense of identity.[26] As we shall see, it is in the telling of personal stories in an empathic environment that identity fragments are drawn together.)

The psychologist Alan Waterman sets identity formation in the context of the way in which the projects of the self provide a person with meaning and purpose. He equates the term 'identity' with 'having a clearly delineated self-definition comprised of those goals, values, and beliefs to which the person is unequivocally committed. These commitments evolve over time and are made because the chosen goals, values, and beliefs are judged worthy of giving a direction, purpose, and meaning to life'.[27]

Erik Erikson provides what I think is still the best theoretical treatment of identity formation available. As is well known, Erikson posits eight stages in the life cycle. The first four relate to infancy and childhood; the fifth is the adolescent stage; and the final three cover the period from young adulthood through to old age. Erikson uses eight sets of polarities to describe the various 'crises' (or turning points): basic trust vs. basic mistrust, autonomy vs. shame and doubt, initiative vs. guilt, industry vs. inferiority, identity vs. identity confusion, intimacy vs. isolation, generativity vs. stagnation, and integrity vs. despair.

Identity is the central focus of his developmental schema. The establishment of a strong sense of 'I' is not viewed simply as the goal of the adolescent stage, but rather as task of the whole of one's life. Erikson showed that the formation of personal identity takes place through a 'fusion of horizons', to use Hans Georg Gadamer's term. On the one hand there is the person's own horizon, her way of viewing herself and her place in the world. On the other hand, there are the perceptions of that person that form the horizons of significant others. In the collision between these horizons a sense of self begins to emerge. 'The sense of ego identity', writes Erikson, 'is the accrued confidence that one's ability to maintain inner sameness and continuity … is matched by the sameness and continuity of one's meaning for others. Thus, self-esteem, confirmed at the end of each major crisis, grows to be a conviction that one is learning effective steps toward a tangible future, that one is developing a defined personality within a social reality which one understands.'[28] It is vitally important for a person to come to a sense that her way of mastering experience is a 'successful variant' on the way significant people around her master experience. Identity formation is a psycho-*social* phenomenon.

Now Erikson's theory of human development has had its critics. Among these have been certain feminist writers. Carol Gilligan, for example, observes that for women intimacy runs alongside identity rather than following it.[29] That is, since relationality – connectedness with others – is the primary way in which a woman engages with life, she comes to a sense of identity through being known. Gilligan further observes that even though Erikson is aware of this reality, he nevertheless persists with his sequence. Thus, she concludes, what we have is a male model of human development.

It may well be that the sequence reflects masculine more than feminine experience. However, two points need to be made here. The first is that Gilligan's linking of relationality with women's experience does not in fact describe the real situation. In their research, Susan Harter and her associates show that it is *gender orientation* rather than gender per se that is predictive of behaviour.[30] That is, one will find a valuing of relationality in both women and men. Secondly, we need to take into account the fact that Erikson's theory includes issues that are prominent in the experience of persons with both a feminine and a masculine gender orientation. Thus, while in the early stages he emphasizes such concerns as autonomy, initiative and task competence, which align more closely with a masculine orientation, in the later crises he focusses on such values as intimacy and care, which feature more strongly in a feminine orientation.

However that may be, there is no doubt that the theory raises a number of issues that are prominent in therapeutic work. Here I am thinking of such issues as shame, guilt, identity confusion, isolation, stagnation or loss of purpose, and despair. In order to develop the idea that empathy contributes to identity formation through knitting together fragmented selves, I will approach Erikson's theory in a fresh way. This will involve thinking about the way in which various subselves or 'subpersonalities' are involved in human development.

The term *subpersonality* comes from the British therapist John Rowan. He was led to form the theory that the personality is made up of a number of subpersonalities by his personal experience.[31] Through Gestalt therapeutic work he found himself discovering various 'aspects' of his personality. Later, he began to realize that these aspects could be grouped together to form subpersonalities. He defines a subpersonality as 'a semi-permanent and semi-autonomous region of the personality capable of acting as a person'.[32]

The term *subself* is more commonly used in the literature, and I will follow this pattern. With this contemporary approach to the self in hand, let us take a new look at Erikson's theory of identity formation. Each crisis in the life cycle can be construed as revolving around the dialectical relationship between two subselves. In the case of the autonomy crisis, the tension is between the autonomous self and the shame-prone self. With reference to the third crisis, the initiative-taking self forms in a dialectical tension with the guilty self. In the school-age phase, the industrious or competent self establishes itself in dialogue with the inferior self. And so on. Identity formation is achieved through the integration of the various selves over time into the superordinate self (the Self).

The way other people interpret the various subselves that make up our Self is, as we have seen, vitally important in this process. It is in the collision between our own self-understanding and the view others have of us that identity is shaped. Those people with a well-formed sense of personal identity have over time integrated the various subselves that have emerged. Moreover, the 'I' that is formed in this way is confirmed by others. Persons suffering from the various forms of psychological dysfunction most often have not been able to achieve this level of integration and self-understanding. They are unable to achieve a wholesome sense of 'I'; rather, their experience of their subjectivity is largely one of fragmentation. There is little cohesion in the way the subselves relate to each other. The pieces simply do not fit together very well; consequently, the sense of self is quite weak.

In therapeutic work, empathy plays the vital role of helping a person overcome this intrapsychic disarray. As Alfred Margulies puts it, the empathic act 'creates a supraordinate recursive structure that enables one to tolerate and knit together fragmented aspects of the self'.[33] The counsellor participates vicariously in the inner world of the other and brings his own view of that to the client. What becomes available is often a view of the client's Self that is more coherent than her own. In this way, the counsellor helps the client draw her various subselves together into a more integrated whole. Margulies describes the process this way:

> Telling one's narrative to another helps one find and constitute oneself. The narrator lives vicariously in the world of the listener as each tries to encounter the other's perspective. The empathizer may give a more coherent viewpoint than the person empathized with may experience, ironically because the empathizer is removed from the frame and has a limited and incomplete view. Paradoxically, this may be clarifying and creative of the self at the same time.[34]

This way of framing the interplay between the counsellor's empathic attunement and the client's sense of self raises the important question of the relationship between *discovery* and *creation* in identity formation.[35] The metaphor of *discovery* suggests that identity formation is fundamentally about coming to know oneself with an ever-increasing level of clarity. In the early stages of the process, both the self and its projects are known only inchoately. The advanced phase of identity formation, however, sees them come much more sharply into focus. It is a process captured by the classical Greek injunctions 'Know thyself' and 'Become what you are'.[36] The premise that such thinking is built on is that the human person is born with an essential self that develops over time.

When the rubric of *creation* is employed in understanding the emergence of a sense of self, identity is viewed primarily as a process in which completely new aspects of personhood are brought into being. The premise here is that there is no essential self. A 'deconstructed self' is an empty space that is filled by the material that is supplied through the interplay of personal choice, on the one hand, and social, cultural and political processes, on the other. Personal identity, according to this view, is something that is constructed by the individual under the impact of socio-political and cultural forces.

Margulies, interestingly, sees both these dynamics at work in empathic interactions. The therapist helps the client to 'find and constitute' his self; she helps him clarify the nature of the drives, abilities, goals and values that are already there. On the other hand, the empathic stance of the therapist is also 'creative of the self'. The therapist has developed her own unique set of perspectives on life in general and on the therapeutic interpretation of it in particular. In forming this collection of perspectives, she has been influenced by certain aspects of the prevailing social, cultural and political environments. Her particular view of reality conditions the form of her empathic attunement. If she has a high empathic capacity she will be able to get very close to the experience of her client. Margulies's point, however, is that she will never be completely within the client's frame of reference. That this is the case is a positive, though, because in this way she is able to contribute something new to his experience of selfhood. She brings a perspective that has the capacity to fill an empty space in the client's self. Something that was not previously there is brought into existence through the empathic act.

The empathic attunement of the therapist contributes significantly, then, to the constitution of the self. Identity is established in relationship. This fact, we have said, provides us with an echo of a central trinitarian dynamic: what it is to be Father, Son and Holy Spirit is fixed in and through the acts of begetting and spirating by the Father (or begetting by the Father, and spirating by the Father and the Son). Now, of course, the principle of identity-through-relationship functions on a different level in trinitarian life from that in the therapeutic relationship. It is not possible to speak about either discovery or creation of identity in relation to the Trinity. The divine persons have their identities fixed through the eternal processes of begetting and spirating. They neither discover nor create their identities; they are constituted through relational processes that exist in the eternal now of the divine life.

There is, naturally enough, a fundamental difference in the nature of the relational activity in the Godhead and in that of the therapeutic encounter. What I have endeavoured to highlight, however, is that the dynamic of identity-through-relationship is foundational in both contexts. Father, Son and Holy Spirit are terms we employ to describe the three relational identities in the Godhead. Begetting and spirating are the processes through which these identities are constituted. Identity is established in relationship. Moreover, the form of this relationship is a loving participation. The particular identity of each divine person is grounded in perfect self-giving. Here we have the model for therapeutic connection with a client through empathy.

Summary

Participation describes the mutual indwelling of the three divine persons. Empathy also involves participation. The empathizer projects herself into the inner world of the client through the imagination. Such sharing in the experience of the other performs the vitally important function of mitigating a deep sense of aloneness. The level of sharing, even for the most perceptive and sensitive of persons, is not maximal. Given that triune participation is total, complete, we have an ideal for empathy. It is important that the counsellor aims for the fullest knowledge and understanding possible.

It is through the participation of the Three that their distinct identities are established. Through the relations of begetting and spirating the being of the persons as Father, as Son and as Holy Spirit is constituted. Identity-through-relations is also an important dynamic in empathic engagement. In stark contrast to the absolute coherence in the being of each of the persons, clients most often struggle with a fragmented sense of self. Through her loving participation in the private world of the client, the counsellor is able to help him overcome this disarray. As the various fragments of the self are knitted together, a stronger sense of identity emerges.

Notes

1   See D. Cunningham, *These Three Are One: The Practice of Trinitarian Theology* (Oxford: Blackwell, 1998), Ch. 5.
2   R.F. Dymond, 'Personality and Empathy', *Journal of Consulting and Clinical Psychology* 14 (1950), pp. 343–50 (p. 344). Cited in C. Duan and C. Hill, 'The Current State of Empathy Research', *Journal of Counseling Psychology* 43:3 (1996), pp. 261–74 (p. 262).
3   J. Zizioulas, *Being as Communion* (Crestwood, NY: St Vladimir's Seminary Press, 1985).
4   See ibid., p. 29ff.
5   See ibid., p. 31.
6   Ibid., pp. 33–34.
7   See ibid., p. 34ff.
8   See ibid., p. 36.
9   Ibid., p. 41.
10 Basil the Great, *De Spiritu Sancto*, trans. B. Jackson, in *A Select Library of Nicene and Post-Nicene Fathers*, vol. 8 (Grand Rapids, Mich.: Eerdmans, 1978), p. 139.
11 See P. Fox, *God as Communion* (Collegeville, Minn.: Liturgical Press, 2001), p. 39.
12 See Cunningham, *These Three Are One*, p. 165.
13 Ibid., p. 115.
14 Ibid., p. 166.
15 G. Egan, *The Skilled Helper*, 4th edn (Pacific Grove, Calif.: Brooks/Cole, 1990), p. 123.
16 The term 'imaginative projection' was used by A. Jenkins in a paper entitled 'Empathy as Dialectic Imagination', delivered at the August 1998 meeting of the American Psychological Association, San Francisco. For a discussion of it, see J. Berecz, 'All that Glitters Is Not Gold: Bad Forgiveness in Counseling and Preaching', *Pastoral Psychology* 49:4 (2001), pp. 253–75 (pp. 259–60).
17 A. Margulies, *The Empathic Imagination* (New York: W.W. Norton, 1989), p. 18.
18 C. Rogers, 'The Necessary and Sufficient Conditions of Therapeutic Personality Change', in H. Kirschenbaum and V. Land Henderson (eds), *The Carl Rogers Reader* (London: Constable, 1990), pp. 219–35 (p. 226).
19 See Cunningham, *These Three Are One*. He posits that along with the virtue of participation, there is also in the triune God the virtue of particularity.
20 C. Rogers, *A Way of Being* (Boston: Houghton Mifflin, 1980), p. 143.
21 See K. Cissna and R. Anderson, 'The Contributions of Carl R. Rogers to a Philosophical Praxis of Dialogue', *Western Journal of Speech Communication* 54 (spring 1990), pp. 125–47 (p. 139).
22 Ibid., p. 139.
23 M. McCarthy, 'Empathy: A Bridge Between', *Journal of Pastoral Care* 46:2 (1992), pp. 119–28 (p. 122).
24 J. Zizioulas, 'On Being a Person: Towards an Ontology of Personhood', in C. Schwobel and C. Gunton (eds), *Persons, Divine and Human* (Edinburgh: T. & T. Clark, 1991), p. 106.
25 T. Cave, 'Fictional Identities', in H. Harris (ed.), *Identity* (Oxford: Clarendon Press, 1995), p. 104.
26 See ibid., pp. 111–12.
27 A. Waterman, 'Identity Formation: Discovery or Creation?' *Journal of Early Adolescence* 4:4 (1984), pp. 329–41 (p. 331).

28   E.H. Erikson, *Identity and the Life Cycle* (New York: International Universities Press, 1959), p. 89.
29   See C. Gilligan, *In a Different Voice: Psychological Theory and Women's Development* (Cambridge, Mass.: Harvard University Press, 1982), p. 12.
30   See S. Harter, *The Construction of the Self: A Developmental Perspective* (New York: Guilford Press, 1999), p. 236ff.
31   See J. Rowan, *Subpersonalities: The People Inside Us* (London: Routledge, 1990), p. 46ff.
32   Ibid., p. 8.
33   Margulies, *The Empathic Imagination*, p. 142.
34   Ibid., pp. 143–4.
35   See Waterman, 'Identity Formation'.
36   See ibid., p. 332.

Chapter 7

Mirroring as an Act of Love

In the previous chapter, we developed a connection between empathy and participation in love. Empathy is the term that Heinz Kohut employs to describe the therapeutic mirroring required to bring healing to clients suffering from narcissistic personality disorder. The argument that I will advance here is that mirroring is an expression of love.

Kohut always wanted to maintain his connection with Freud and the psychoanalytic tradition. However, as Kohut's understanding of self psychology developed, central Freudian planks such as drive theory, unconscious conflict and the aim of ego dominance became less and less important to him.[1] Self psychology emerged out of Kohut's work with patients suffering with narcissistic personality disorder. These are patients dominated by feelings of emptiness, meaninglessness and shame. Kohut found that what they need most is to be accepted and admired. The affirmation and admiration he offered to his patients he referred to as 'mirroring'.

Donald Capps has taken up the concept of positive mirroring and demonstrated its pastoral significance. Capps also provides some interesting and enlightening theological reflection on mirroring.[2] He works with two biblical stories containing strong affirming actions, namely, the account of the woman who anointed Jesus's feet (Luke 7:36–50), and the Johannine version of the crucifixion scene in which Jesus 'gives' his mother and the beloved disciple to each other (John 19:26–7). In this chapter, the theological analysis will take a different shape: it will involve the use of the doctrine of the Trinity. The particular approach taken will include the analogical move developed by Augustine and Aquinas. The analogical method consists of the attempt to locate an element of human experience that reflects the nature of God's life and love. Through his reflection on the affirming actions of Jesus, Capps shows how mirroring replaces 'the bond of shame' with the 'bond of love'.[3] I want to build on this important insight. Triune love is one and it is three. The unity in the meaning of the divine love is found in God's gift of God's self for the world. This loving self-communication is, however, expressed in three ways: the Father is the Originating Lover; the Son is the incarnation of that Love; and the Spirit is the living power of that Love available in the world. In making the analogical move, I will suggest that human love is also one and three. Our love is always a communion between lover and beloved in which each one wants the best for the other. While there is this unity in the meaning of human love, it also has three distinct forms: agape, eros and philia. With this in mind, I want to argue the thesis that positive mirroring is an act of love in which agapic, erotic and philial elements are all expressed. The fullness of divine love is expressed in and through the participation of Father, Son and Holy Spirit. There is no division or separation in divine loving, but there is particularity. Each person manifests the divine love in a particular way. In the agapic, erotic and philial love expressed by the pastoral counsellor in and through her mirroring, we see an image of the love of the triune God.

The nature of God's love, along with the analogical approach in trinitarian theology, will need to be discussed in order to illuminate this line of thinking. Before getting to this, however, it is necessary to describe Kohut's notion of mirroring and to offer reasons for my assertion that here we find a therapeutic expression of love.

Narcissism and Mirroring

In the psychotherapeutic literature, narcissism is usually referred to as the least severe of the 'borderline conditions'. This term is used to denote a loose collection of characterological disorders that can be located on the border between neuroses and psychoses. Unlike the patients with neuroses, people diagnosed with borderline disorders suffer from a fragmentation of the self. In other words, such persons have a poorly formed ego. People with borderline disorders can be distinguished from those experiencing psychotic symptoms through the fact that the former are definitely in contact with reality.

The main characteristics of narcissistic personality disorder are a pervasive pattern of grandiosity, a tendency to exaggerate accomplishments, hypersensitivity to criticism, and a lack of empathy with others.[4] Kohut reports that narcissistic patients commonly describe themselves as not feeling 'fully real' but rather as feeling empty and depressed.[5] They talk about their emotions being dulled and about the fact that they simply go through the motions of life. Their sense of self-worth is low and they experience little joy in, or zest for, living. In order to defend against these feelings of self-depletion and worthlessness, they engage in grandiose behaviour:

> Behind [the grandiosity] lie low self-esteem and depression – a deep sense of uncared-for worthlessness and rejection, an incessant hunger for response, a yearning for reassurance. All in all, the excited hypervitality of the patient must be understood as an attempt to counteract through self-stimulation a feeling of inner deadness and depression.[6]

Kohut contends that the root cause of the very weak sense of self in patients diagnosed with narcissistic personality disorder can be found in childhood experiences of extreme empathic failures on the part of self-objects (the term refers to the fact that the object – a parent – is experienced as part of the self). It is not the case, however, that the emerging self needs perfect empathic attunement from parents in order to become strong and vital. Indeed, 'optimal frustration' serves the purpose of the laying down of self-esteem regulating psychological structure. When there is a small-scale empathic failure (for instance, mother is on the phone and can't respond immediately to baby's needs), the infant borrows the self-esteem regulating function of the parent. This process Kohut refers to as 'transmuting internalisation'.[7] The developing self needs to internalize the self-soothing function in order to be strong enough to cope with the empathic failures that are an inevitable part of interpersonal relationships in later life.

Kohut uses the term 'a cohesive self' to describe the person who is able to engage robustly and joyfully with the tasks and challenges of life. Cohesion in the self exists when there is a relative harmony between talents and ambitions on the one hand, and ideals and goals on the other. Kohut posits a bipolar view of the self: a grandiose and an idealizing self.[8] The poles correspond to two basic psychological functions, namely, 'healthy self-assertiveness vis-à-vis the mirroring self-object', and 'healthy admiration for the idealized self-object'. Healthy psychological functioning across both sectors is described through the use of the metaphor of a 'tension arc'.[9] The inner spark of the person suffering from narcissistic personality disorder is too weak to set up the tension arc. She is unable to employ her talents and pursue her goals, and in consequence finds herself beset by feelings of emptiness, depression and shame.

Shame – the feeling that one is inferior, flawed – is a prominent feature in the symptomatology of the patient diagnosed with narcissistic personality disorder. Andrew Morrison argues that it is, in fact, the *primary* affect associated with narcissism.[10] That this is the case alerts pastoral practitioners to the fact that we are dealing with a widespread phenomenon (at least when one includes the milder expressions). Writers on shame tell us that it is all around us. Robert Karen reports that 'many psychologists now believe that shame is the preeminent cause of emotional distress in our time'.[11] Positive mirroring, the antidote to shame, is therefore of vital importance for the pastoral ministry.

Kohut suggests that the admiring, affirming, approving stance of the therapist, over time, facilitates increased self-acceptance and a higher level of self-esteem. Such mirroring is expressed through empathic attunement. The therapist must be able to think and feel herself consistently into the inner world of experience of her client in order to communicate understanding and acceptance. Kohut provides this outline of the healing process: (1) Optimal frustration in the mirror transference resulting from inevitable small-scale empathic failures leads to (2) transmuting internalization, which results in (3) the laying down of the missing psychological structure.[12] When the mental structure is built up the self becomes more cohesive, and a more cohesive self allows for self-esteem regulation in the face of one's own failures and the assaults of others. A stronger, more integrated self also means that there is relative harmony between its grandiose and idealizing sectors.

Now my argument is that positive mirroring is an act of love in which agape, eros and philia all have a role. Before supplying my reasons for this assertion, I need to describe love and its forms.

Love is One and Love is Three

The starting point in any analysis of love is the recognition of the unity in its meaning. As Paul Tillich puts it, 'love is one'.[13] Love in all its forms, he contends, is the drive toward the reunion of the separated. Love functions to unite 'that which is self-centered and individual'.[14] Tillich shaped his theology in dialogue with existential philosophy, and a central concept in that philosophy is estrangement or alienation. When our existence is marked by sin, he contends, we experience alienation from self, others and God.[15] Love is the power that allows the human person to overcome this state of estrangement.

Taking my cue from Tillich, I suggest that the primary aim of love is the establishment of a state of communion. Love is communion between lover and beloved in which each one wants the best for the other and actively seeks it. Edward Vacek follows a similar line in his attempt to capture the unity in the meaning of love: 'Love is an affective, affirming participation in the goodness of a being (or Being).'[16] The three forms of love, each in their own distinct way, aim to establish communion.

Agape is self-giving for the sake of the other. Jesus teaches us to turn the other cheek, to walk the extra mile, to love our enemies. Gene Outka's term for this kind of love is 'equal regard'.[17] Friend or enemy, intelligent or dull, attractive or not – everyone is deserving of our respect, consideration and care. Anders Nygren, in his discussion of agape, refers time and again to the fact that it is sovereign and not dependent, spontaneous and not motivated.[18] We who are agapists are not compelled to love; we choose to love. We are not driven by the thought of personal gain; we are moved by the love of God being channelled through us.

All of us find it easy to love those we experience as attractive. Agapists find a way to love the unlovable. They may not feel like loving, but they have a strong enough will to make it happen. Vacek agrees that will plays a central role in expressing agape. But he does not want to take the idea that love transcends negative feelings to mean that emotion is unimportant. 'When our action originates in emotion, we are more fully engaged in our acts and not simply "going through the motions". We love only when we have been *moved* and *attracted* to affirm the beloved's (real and ideal) goodness' (emphasis in the original).[19] That emotion makes a vital contribution to agape is important in the context of mirroring, as we shall see in more detail below. An admiring and approving stance that is just going through the motions is not a real antidote to shame and emptiness.

The second form of love is *eros*. Webster's dictionary uses the following terms to describe this type of love: 'ardent desire', 'yearning' and 'aspiring self-fulfilling love often having a sensuous quality'. Eros is a desire, but it is not limited to sexual desire. It is 'a creative energy, the life force, the unifier, the creative urge in nature and the human spirit'.[20] In Greek philosophy, it is construed as the desire, the drive, to participate fully in knowledge and in the good. For St Augustine, it is the power that drives people towards God. 'My heart is restless', he wrote in the *Confessions*, 'and it will not rest until it rests in you.' The desire of eros to ascend to the heights of human experience and beyond that to the life of the divine is grounded in self-love. The person in the grip of eros knows that such an ascent is the path to self-fulfilment. It is not an egoistic love, however, for while the good of the self is primary, it is not the exclusive focus.

Eros, then, is a yearning for union with the true, the good, the beautiful and, ultimately, the divine. It is a power that attracts. 'The essence of eros is that it draws us from ahead … Something in me responds to the other person … and pulls me toward him.'[21] Though I seek to find my fulfilment in and through the other (whether it is another person, the good, or the divine), the other is not simply an object for me. I have a genuine interest in, and concern for, the other. Eros is not lust. Eros is not abuse of the other. It is a form of love that connects the self to its urges and needs, but it does so without closing it in on itself.

Philia, finally, is a mutual love. It is expressed in the reciprocity of friendship. Philia draws people together; it is the power that creates union and builds community. Jesus referred to an agapic love through which one lays downs one's life for others, but these others are no longer strangers, but friends (John 15:13). Those who have come to know and embrace this love of God in Christ are drawn by the Spirit into a community, Christ's Body. Vacek helpfully draws the contrast between philia and the other two loves:

> Philia is distinguished from agape and eros by the *mutuality* of the relation it creates. In philia, as in all love, we love our beloveds. But in philia we love them not for their own sake, as separate individuals, nor for our sake ..., but for the sake of the mutual relationship we share with them.[22]

Philia is a mutual love. It is the good of the relationship that is the primary concern for philial lovers.

Having mapped the territory of love, it is now necessary to indicate where positive mirroring is located on this map. I will begin by connecting it with love via affirmation and communion. And then I will attempt to show how mirroring incorporates the three loves.

Mirroring as an Act of Love

Kohut contrasts the reaction the narcissist experiences in the face of rejection and disapproval with the reaction produced through mirroring: 'Instead of a pleasant suffusion of the body surface, there is the heat of unpleasant blushing; instead of a pleasurable confirmation of the value, beauty, and *loveableness of the self*, there is painful shame' (emphasis added).[23] What the shame-prone person needs most is to know that she is lovable. Technique cannot deliver a feeling that one is lovable; neither will psychotherapeutic knowledge. Only love can communicate to a person that she is lovable. Moreover, it needs to be a love that goes beyond will to incorporate emotion. As we saw earlier, the other person does not feel loved when he senses that one is simply going through the motions. Mirroring responses that are disconnected from the emotions of the counsellor sound empty. The narcissistic client will appreciate the good intention behind the affirming statements, but in the end he will experience them as yet another form of rejection. What he needs is for the counsellor to connect with him at the level of both the head and the heart. What he needs is not simply mirroring words but a mirroring love. Affirmation and love go together. 'Love is affirmation. The affirmative (*ad-firmare*: "to give firmness to" or "to strengthen") nature of love clarifies love's power to change its object.'[24]

Love and communion also go together. This is why 'communion' is offered as the key word in my statement of the unity in the meaning of love. Mirroring makes communion possible. 'Positive mirroring engenders love, and of such love community is born.'[25] Scott Peck offers a case study involving a client called Marcia that illustrates very clearly the indissoluble link between love, communion and mirroring. He recalls that after a year of therapy his client asked him a question he found very threatening:

'Do you think I'm a bit of a shit?' asked Marcia .... With my heart pounding I went out on what seemed to be a very shaky limb indeed. 'Marcia', I said, 'you have been seeing me now for over a year. During this long period of time things have not gone smoothly for us. Much of the time we have been struggling, and the struggle has often been boring or nerve-racking or angry for both of us. Yet despite this you have continued to come back to see me at considerable effort and inconvenience to you, session after session, week after week, month after month. You wouldn't have been able to do this unless you were the kind of person who is determined to grow and willing to work hard at making yourself a better person. I do not think I would feel that someone who works as hard on herself as you do is a bit of a shit. So the answer is, No, I do not think you are a bit of a shit. In fact, I admire you a great deal.[26]

Peck goes on to say that with Marcia (and with other clients) it is the mutual commitment to the struggle to find healing and growth that is critical in the counselling experience. Letting the client know that you like and admire her has an important role to play only because it comes in the context of a deep and real relationship. It is the communion that is established in love that is the heart of therapy. '[What is critical] is the willingness of the therapist to extend himself or herself for the purpose of nurturing the patient's growth – willingness to go out on a limb, to truly involve oneself at an emotional level in the relationship, to actually struggle with the patient and with oneself. In short, the essential ingredient of successful deep and meaningful psychotherapy is love.'[27]

The agapic element in mirroring is expressed through this extension of the self. The therapist needs to stretch herself, to give of herself in attuning to the experience of the client. For Kohut, it is the empathic participation of the therapist that communicates acceptance and affirmation. She needs to attend closely and intensely to the client in order to think and feel into his inner life. This attending requires emotional and mental energy and is ultimately an expression of love. The 'optimal frustration' precipitated by small-scale empathic failures on the part of the therapist is the catalyst for the laying down of psychological structure. The frustration is *optimal* only because the therapist has demonstrated a loving extension of herself through empathic attunement. There can be no mirroring without agapic attentiveness and understanding.

Mirroring also has an eros component. Recall that eros involves an attraction; it is the desire for someone (or something) to help one attain self-realization. We need to ask what it is that attracts the therapist in working with narcissists. It needs to be said at the outset that it is almost always the case that they are experienced as very difficult and demanding people to work with. They are needy, fragile, grandiose and angry. Beth, a member of my congregation, was all of those things. I struggled hard with Beth in our sessions together. The search for ways to mirror her in a congruent manner consumed me. After about a year of regular and intense pastoral contact, Beth asked me to make another visit. When I arrived, I found her in a very excitable state. She told me that she wanted to take on leadership of the music ministry and she put up an outlandish programme for how she would do it. Though she was a talented musician, her psychological dysfunction meant that she could never effectively take on such a leadership role. Shocked and dismayed, I wondered how to respond. I began by affirming her musical gifts, and then went on to say that I did not think she had the gift of leadership. At that point, she quietened down and for the first time let go of her grandiose defence and spoke out of her real self. That is, she spoke out of her fragile, shame-prone self. 'How would anyone know that?' she said very quietly and with deep sadness. 'No one has ever given me a chance.' I told her that I would love to give her a chance, but I didn't think it would be good for her or for the church in the long run. After a short period of further conversation I took my leave. I fully expected Beth to react with narcissistic rage. I left wondering why that didn't in fact happen. She just needed some time, it seems. The next morning she telephoned me and raged as violently against me as anyone ever has. After enduring half an hour of abuse I decided to end the conversation.

For quite a long time she did not ask to see me. When next she did make that request, I observed that something had changed in me. That one moment in which she related to me in a real and honest way touched something in me. I found that I was much more relaxed and my mirroring came with much less effort. There seemed to be a new level in our relationship. In the period that followed Beth was calmer and more joyful than I had ever seen her.

If working with narcissists is often so frustrating and painful, how is it attractive? Where is the eros element in the relationship? What pulls the therapist, I suggest, is both the struggle and the commitment the client brings to that struggle. Sportspersons love a competition and therapists love a struggle. As is the case with competitive sport, there is in the mirror transference pain, frustration and disappointment. There is also a deep sense of satisfaction and fulfilment that comes with working through it. One finds oneself drawn into the challenging and demanding work of empathic attunement. There is a pull, too, to work through the difficult moments associated with 'optimal frustration' and the concomitant break in the rapport with the client. Working through the mirror transference is a very large challenge – we need that challenge. And we find real fulfilment in seeing the fruits of, on the one hand, the personal and professional gifts we bring and, on the other, the courage, vulnerability and perseverance the client brings.

We noted above that eros for the Greeks was thought of as a passionate desire for knowledge. This expression of eros is also found in therapy. There it is not so much a drive for intellectual mastery, though, as it is a deep attraction to the complexities and richness in the psychic life of an individual. A good therapist is fascinated by the personal story that is unfolding before him or her. He or she experiences a strong pull towards understanding as fully as possible the way inner and outer life is experienced by the client. A very good example of this is provided by Otto Rank in his therapeutic work with Anaïs Nin.[28] I will attempt to show that Nin suffered from a narcissistic disturbance and that, further, Rank's eagerness to understand her psychic life was experienced by her as positive mirroring.

Anaïs Nin was born in Neuilly, a suburb of Paris. As a child she accompanied her father, the famous Spanish composer-pianist Joaquín Nin, on concert tours all over Europe. In her teens, long after her father had left the family, she broke out of the demoralizing confines of a poor existence with her Danish-born mother in New York to become an artists' model and, later, a Spanish dancer. As a novice writer, she made her way back to Paris with its literary and cultural atmosphere. In 1929 she settled at Louveciennes and there, as in her apartment in New York's Greenwich Village after the outbreak of World War II, she welcomed a host of little-known (though destined to be famous) creative people.

In her journals, we find, among other things, a record of her experiences in therapy with Rank and with her first analyst, René Allendy, the founder of the French Psychoanalytic Society. While one recognizes that it is not possible to develop psychological categories with any degree of certainty from a collection of remarks and reflections in a personal journal (even one as detailed as Nin's), it does seem possible to identify a number of quite clear indications of (a mild at least) narcissistic disturbance. As we have seen, the symptoms of the disorder are inferiority feelings, propensity for embarrassment, shame, depression and a feeling of not being fully real. We also saw that Kohut attributes the condition to acute empathic failures on the part of self-objects. An indication that Anaïs Nin suffered with narcissistic personality disorder is found in an entry in her journal referring to inferiority feelings. She identifies a lack of self-confidence as a major source of distress in her life:

> [With Dr. Allendy] I talked about my work, and my life in general. I said I had always been very independent and had never leaned on anyone. Dr. Allendy said, 'In spite of that, you seem to lack confidence.' He had touched a sensitive spot. Confidence![29]

This lack of confidence she relates to her figure. She feels inferior when she compares herself with women who are well endowed. Men love only 'big, healthy women with enormous breasts', she laments.[30] She recalls the Spanish proverb quoted often by her mother, 'Bones are for the dogs.' To compensate for what she perceives as physical undesirability, she decided early to shape her persona around her artistic gifts. 'It was to forget this [a petite body] that I decided to be an artist, or writer, to be interesting, charming, accomplished. I was not sure of being beautiful enough.'[31]

A further indication of narcissism is the way in which Nin recalls for her analyst the painful experience associated with the extreme empathic failures of her father:

> My father did not want a girl. My father was over-critical. He was never satisfied, never pleased. I never remember a compliment or a caress from him. At home, only scenes, quarrels, beatings. And his hard blue eyes on us, looking for flaws. When I was ill with typhoid fever, almost dying, all he could say was: 'Now you are ugly, how ugly you are.'[32]

We have seen that in reaction to these traumatic childhood narcissistic injuries a person usually develops an intense craving for affirmation and approval. This was certainly the case with Anaïs Nin. She acknowledges her fear of being hurt and laments over the associated need for constant confirmation of affection. 'I despise my own hypersensitiveness', she writes, 'which requires so much reassurance. It is certainly abnormal to crave so much to be loved and understood.'[33] In order to develop a full and accurate picture of a person's psychopathology it is necessary to spend many hours in face-to-face conversation. All we have before us is a small collection of personal, psychologically oriented reflections. And yet one cannot help but be struck by the appearance of a number of classic symptoms of narcissistic personality disorder.

Sadly, it seems that Allendy only aggravated Nin's narcissistic injury. He failed to understand her fully, and was too quick to pour her into the mould of his psychoanalytic theories. She compares this reductionistic approach with the openness and insight in Rank's style:

> 'I felt that Dr. Allendy's formulas did not fit my life. I have read all your books. I felt that there is *more* in my relationship to my father than the desire of a victory over my mother.'
>
> By his smile I knew he [Rank] understood the *more* and my objection to oversimplification
> ...
> Immediately I knew that we talked the same language. He said, 'I go beyond the psychoanalytical. Psychoanalysis emphasizes the resemblance between people; I emphasize the differences between people. They try to bring everybody to a certain normal level. I try to adapt each person to his own kind of universe.'[34]

This appreciation of her uniqueness that Rank showed reflected his passionate interest in Nin and her psychic life. 'He was agile, quick', she writes, 'as if each word I uttered were a precious object he had excavated and was delighted to find. He acted as if I were unique, as if this were a unique adventure, not a phenomenon to be categorized.'[35] Otto Rank provides us with a good example of the therapist who is driven by a desire to understand his client as fully as possible. This is the eros element at work. The therapist comes alive in the encounter with the client and the thoughts and feelings that are shared. Moreover, his passionate interest in the client provides a powerful source of affirmation. Anaïs Nin clearly valued very deeply the fact that her words were 'precious' to Rank and that the discoveries associated with them brought him delight.

I referred above to the give and take that characterizes the counselling relationship. It is here that we find the philial element. To be sure, there cannot be a mutuality in self-disclosure. We do not find the total reciprocity that is characteristic of friendship. But there is nevertheless reciprocity. Alastair Campbell describes quite beautifully the mutuality in professional caring relationships through the use of the terms 'gift, gratitude and grace'.[36] Both the counsellor and the client give gifts in the experience they share in. The relationship reaches its full potential when both are able to receive that which is offered with gratitude and grace.

Philia is friendship love. Three central elements in a friendship are these: a desire to spend time together; reciprocity (there is give and take); and a commitment to the health of the relationship. In the bond of love forged through the mirror transference these three elements are present. This relationship does not constitute friendship in an unqualified sense, however. Friendship in the full sense requires the presence of a fourth factor, namely deep affection. While it is sometimes the case that the partners in a therapeutic relationship experience strongly affectionate feelings, it is not always so. The desire to be together is associated not so much with personal attractiveness as with the important work that is being done in and through the counselling. Campbell refers to the 'moderated love' in a professional caring relationship.[37] This is a real love, but it is a love that operates within certain bounds. It is different in quality from the love shared between friends and family members. The bond developed through the philial love in the mirror transference could perhaps be referred to as a 'moderated friendship'. It is vitally important that this element of friendship is present in the mirroring work of the counsellor. Attempts to affirm and prize the client that are grounded in technique rather than in personal giving are bound to be ineffective. The client needs to experience the tonality of friendship in mirror communications if they are to be received as genuine.

In summary, positive mirroring is an act of love. Not only is love present, it is present in its agapic, erotic and philial forms. Here, I believe, we have a reflection of the love of the Trinity. God's love is one and it is three.

An Analogy with the 'Trinity of Love'

In his book *The Trinity of Love*, Tony Kelly uses an analogical approach in which, as the title suggests, love is central. God does not simply engage in loving actions, God *is* love. It is in the very nature of God to offer Godself to the world. We who know God reflect God's love. 'Christian existence is a dynamic image of the divine reality of self-giving love.'[38]

Kelly's approach is an extension of the analogical work of Augustine and Aquinas. In *De Trinitate*, Augustine, as we have already seen (Chapter 1) draws upon a range of psychological images to assist us in understanding the nature of triune life. He refers to the lover, the beloved and the love; to the mind, its knowledge and its love; and to memory, understanding and will. The reason, he thinks, why these images are so helpful in gaining insight into trinitarian relations is that they represent imprints of the divine. A vitally important image for Augustine is the last mentioned of the three above. The three psychological faculties of memory, understanding and will are distinct and yet there is a mutual indwelling. The interrelationship exists because there is a 'mutual comprehension', and this mutual comprehension in turns indicates a fundamental equality between the faculties.

> Whatever of intelligible things that I do remember and will, it follows that I also understand. My will also comprehends my whole understanding and my whole memory, if only I make use of the whole of what I understand and remember. Wherefore, when all are mutually comprehended by each one, and are comprehended as wholes, then each one as a whole is equal to each other one as a whole, and each one as a whole is equal to all together as wholes; and these three are one life, one mind, and one essence.
>
> (Augustine X.11, 18)[39]

Aquinas also develops a psychological analogy in constructing his theology of the Trinity. He begins the *Summa*, however, by reflecting on the meaning of God considered as a unity. As with all his theology, he uses Aristotelian ontological categories. For Aquinas, God is the sheer act of being. 'God is self-subsistent being itself.'[40] 'God is his own essence' and 'he is also his own existence'.[41] It is not that God participates in being; God *is* being. Later in the *Summa*, Aquinas turns his attention to the trinitarian nature of God. In his approach to the Trinity, as we saw in Chapter 1, a key term is *procession*. There are two processions in God. These are the procession of the Word, which Aquinas calls generation or begetting, and the procession of Love, which he refers to as 'spiration' ('breathing out').[42] In order to help clarify the nature of these processions, Aquinas draws analogies with intellect, will, and love:

One must bear in mind that in God procession corresponds only to an action which remains within the agent himself, not to one bent on something external. In the spiritual world the only actions of this kind are those of the intellect and the will. But the Word's procession corresponds to the action of the intellect. Now in us there is another spiritual process following the action of the will, namely the coming forth of love, whereby what is loved is in the lover, just as the thing expressed or actually understood in the conceiving of an idea is in the knower. For this reason besides the procession of the Word another procession is posited in God, namely the procession of Love.[43]

Kelly contends that it is necessary to go beyond Aquinas's idea of God as the sheer act of Being to one of God as the sheer act of love. Grounding his approach in the Johannine corpus, he builds the notion of the Trinity as 'Being-in-Love' (here he borrows Bernard Lonergan's term):

For God gives the world, seemingly incurably ignorant and hostile to both love and God, what he most loves, what is most intimate to his own identity, the Son. In giving the Son, God is manifested as Loving self-involvement in history. In communicating the Spirit, such love establishes the Christian in the ultimate dimension of life and truth: the divine 'Being-in-Love'.[44]

The unity in the meaning of divine love is found in God's self-communication to the world. But this loving donation that God makes also has its distinct forms:

To say that God is Father is to say that God is 'from God': the Love that God is comes from nowhere else, no one else. It is pure originality, pure self-giving. To say that God is Son and Word, is to say that Love is 'of God', infinite in its self-expression and self-communication: it is beyond the finite, and expresses itself as the divine meaning and value of God, and all else that might come into existence to receive it. To say that God is Spirit, is to say that Love is communicated 'as God': God's gifts and loving are not finite; they terminate in a perfect communion within God and with God; 'in the unity of the Holy Spirit'.[45]

I am suggesting that the love that is expressed through positive mirroring is a reflection of the 'Trinity of Love'. It is also one and three. The unity in the meaning of mirror love is that it is self-giving through empathic participation in the inner world of experience of the other. But it also has its distinct expressions. The love that the counsellor offers in the mirror transference is agapic, erotic and philial.

Summary

It is not common for psychotherapists and counsellors to use the word 'love' to describe the work that they do. To talk of love is to shift the ground from the scientific and the professional to the intangible and the religious. Such a move tends to make them very uncomfortable. The argument advanced here, however, has been that in relation to positive mirroring it is necessary and right to speak of a loving commitment. In order to help the narcissistic person feel lovable one needs to find love inside oneself. Forging the empathic connection that is required to bring healing and growth is motivated by love. The unity in the meaning of this love is expressed in the idea of self-communication. It has also been argued that this self-giving has three forms: agape, eros and philia. Here we find an image of Love of the Father, Son, and Holy Spirit.

Notes

1   See H. Kohut, *The Restoration of the Self* (New York: International Universities Press, 1977); idem, *How Does Analysis Cure?* (Chicago: University of Chicago Press, 1984).
2   See D. Capps, *The Depleted Self* (Minneapolis: Fortress Press, 1993), pp. 162–7.
3   See ibid., p. 165.
4   See ibid., p. 12.
5   See H. Kohut, *The Analysis of the Self* (New York: International Universities Press, 1971), p. 16.
6   Kohut, *The Restoration of the Self*, p. 5.
7   See Kohut, *The Analysis of the Self*, p. 49.
8   See Kohut, *The Restoration of the Self*, p. 177.
9   See ibid., p. 178.
10   See A.P. Morrison, 'Shame, Ideal Self, and Narcissism', in A.P. Morrison (ed.), *Essential Papers on Narcissism* (New York University Press, 1986), pp. 348–71.
11   R. Karen, 'Shame', *Atlantic Monthly* (Feb. 1992), pp. 40–70 (p. 40).
12   See Kohut, *How Does Analysis Cure?*, pp. 98–9.
13   P. Tillich, *Love, Power and Justice* (Oxford University Press, 1954), p. 27.
14   Ibid., p. 26.
15   See P. Tillich, *Systematic Theology*, vol. 2 (University of Chicago Press, 1957), p. 44ff.
16   E. Vacek, *Love, Human and Divine: The Heart of Christian Ethics* (Washington, DC: Georgetown University Press, 1994), p. 34.
17   See G. Outka, *Agape: An Ethical Analysis* (New Haven, Conn.: Yale University Press, 1972).
18   See A. Nygren, *Agape and Eros*, parts I and II (London: SPCK, 1932, 1939).
19   Vacek, *Love, Human and Divine*, p. 162.
20   P. Avis, *Eros and the Sacred* (London: SPCK, 1989), p. 129.
21   R. May, *Love and Will* (London: Souvenir Press, 1970), p. 129.
22   Vacek, *Love, Human and Divine*, p. 281.
23   H. Kohut, *The Search for the Self*, ed. P. Ornstein (New York: International Universities Press, 1978), p. 439.
24   Vacek, *Love, Human and Divine*, p. 56.
25   Capps, *The Depleted Self*, p. 165.
26   M.S. Peck, *The Road Less Travelled* (London: Arrow Books, 1990), pp. 183–4 [first published 1978].
27   Ibid., p. 186.
28   I used this case study in Chapter 8 of my book *The Art of Listening: Dialogue, Shame, and Pastoral Care* (Grand Rapids, Mich.: Eerdmans, 2002). There my interest was different, however. I cited Dr Allendy's approach to Anaïs Nin as an example of therapeutic disconfirmation.
29   A. Nin, *The Journals of Anaïs Nin, 1931–1934*, ed. G. Stuhlmann (London: Peter Owen, 1966), pp. 75–6.
30   Ibid., p. 81.
31   Ibid., p. 81.

32   Ibid., p. 76.
33   Ibid., p. 77.
34   Ibid., p. 271.
35   Ibid., p. 272.
36   A. Campbell, *Moderated Love: A Theology of Professional Care* (London: SPCK, 1984), pp. 106–7.
37   See ibid.
38   A. Kelly, *The Trinity of Love* (Wilmington, Del.: Michael Glazier, 1989), p. 146.
39   Augustine, *The Trinity*, trans. S. McKenna (Boston: St Paul Editions, 1965), pp. 200–201.
40   Aquinas, *Summa Theologiae*, Ia.4.2. I have used the edition trans. by T. Gilby (London: Eyre & Spottiswoode, 1964–5).
41   Aquinas, *Summa*, Ia.3.4.
42   Aquinas, *Summa*, Ia.2.1–5.
43   Aquinas, *Summa*, Ia.27.3.
44   Kelly, *The Trinity of Love*, p. 147.
45   Ibid., p. 178.

CONCLUDING WITH THEODICY

Chapter 8

The Trinity and Suffering

In our discussions of the various issues that have cropped up throughout this book, we have met a number of people for whom suffering is a major factor in their lives. Remember Candice? She is the little girl confronted by the pain of illness and the strangeness of hospitalization. Ruth, too, faces a battle with illness. That horrible disease, multiple sclerosis, besets her. For Beth, suffering enters not through physical but mental dysfunction. She struggles with narcissistic personality disorder. David, finally, is living under the dark cloud of depression. We have explored a number of important techniques and strategies for helping these individuals, and others like them. We have also been mindful, however, of the fact that the foundation stones of care are personal presence and empathy.

When people are hurting they greatly appreciate the understanding and support that others offer. It is comforting to know that there are those who care and understand. For Christians who are suffering, though, there is another reality. They also seek comfort from their God. It is common to ask the question, Where is God in this? We want God to bring the healing and relief that we have been praying for. In the meantime, we want to know that God is feeling with us in our pain. Alfred North Whitehead gives expression to an image of the divine for which many feel a need. For him, God is 'the great companion – the fellow-sufferer who understands'.[1] The two arenas of care, the human and the divine, are closely linked. Our empathy can point suffering people to divine empathy. 'Sympathetic caring conveys the religious truth that God shoulders the cross of the sufferer as well ... God does not exempt the Godhead from the order of things, but identifies with the burdens and sorrows of humanity.'[2]

To know that God suffers with us is a rich source of consolation. But is it in fact true that God 'shoulders our cross' with us? Is God really a 'fellow-sufferer'? Until quite recently, virtually all theologians recoiled from such a view. For all but the very recent history of Christian thought the doctrine of the impassibility of God has reigned supreme. The thinking ran like this. God is the 'unmoved Mover', and since to suffer means being influenced or 'moved' by something outside the self, God cannot suffer. God is perfection, and as suffering involves change God must be exempt. How can a perfect Being change? (Impassibility and immutability are two sides of the one coin.) God is love and mercy and acts to relieve our suffering, but God cannot suffer with us.

In recent times, we have witnessed a revolt against this kind of thinking. The apathetic God, many contend, seems more like a rock than the personal God of the Bible. In the wake of the agonies and atrocities of the last century – the Holocaust sitting right at the centre – most theologians have found it impossible to accept the notion of a God who sits aloof in heavenly bliss. God must be right there in the midst of our pain and distress. Even so, there have been some influential voices wanting to uphold the traditional view of an impassible God. Some have even argued that a God who does not suffer is more loving, more compassionate, than one who does.[3] To introduce suffering into the divine life is to bring a change. And change can only weaken the perfect love and mercy of God.

Pastoral carers are, on the whole, instinctively inclined to the current view that God suffers. Compassion and empathy are at the forefront of our ministry. When we encounter those who are hurting, we enter into their pain. We suffer with them, though in an attenuated manner. It is difficult for us to conceive of a God who is compassionate but who at the same time is sealed off from our suffering. Indeed, I shall be using pastoral insights to help guide us through the theological landscape of the question of divine suffering. Here the work of the French philosopher Gabriel Marcel will feature. Marcel talks about interpersonal relationships in terms of availability and its counterfeit, 'constancy'. To be available to another person is to be receptive, to be 'porous'. The experience of the other must be able to find its way into my being. On the other hand, it is quite possible to act for the good of the other without receptivity. I simply do my duty while holding myself back from her inner experience. This is constancy – a pretend form of availability. By analogy, for God to be truly available to us, God must participate fully in our lot. To act benevolently without entering into our experience would be to fall into constancy.

This is already sounding very 'heady'. Suffering people will not be helped by intellectual arguments concerning God's participation in their pain. If we are to lead others with integrity, however, to the 'fellow-sufferer who understands', we had better check whether such a one actually exists.

Theologians who argue for a suffering God usually locate the cross at the centre of their reflections. Here we see a 'crucified God'. The passion and death of Jesus is a trinitarian event. Father and Son are caught up together in the pain of Golgotha. Some who argue against divine passibility also turn to the doctrine of the Trinity. As we follow the debate, then, we will be led into trinitarian thinking.

As I have been implying, my pastoral inclination takes me in the direction of a suffering God. I want to argue for an empathic God, for a God who suffers and who is able to feel with us in our pain. But first let us consider the views of those who argue for a compassionate God who is at the same time impassible.

An Impassible God?

The line to contemporary theologians who argue against a suffering God starts with Plato and Aristotle and passes through Thomas Aquinas. In the cosmology of the Greek philosophers, the immutable substances are separated from the material ones. The realm of Being has no contact with the realm of Becoming. The Highest Substance, God, cannot enter into a relationship with the transient world. For God to make contact with the world of change, becoming would have to enter God's reality.

Aquinas works with this world-view. A fundamental starting point in his theology is that God does not change (God is 'immutable'). God is 'the unchanging first cause of change'.[4] All material substances are subject to the process of becoming. They have a potential that is actualized in this transient process. God, however, is 'sheer actuality' (*actus purus*). 'In the first existent thing everything must be actual; there can be no potentiality whatsoever.'[5] This does not mean that in God something has been fully actualized; God is actuality pure and simple.

Now something is perfect when it has achieved actuality. It has moved from the state of potentiality to actuality and has thereby fulfilled itself. In this sense, it has reached perfection. God is pure actuality and therefore perfect.[6] Everything else requires an origin for its existence. But God is self-subsistent being itself (*ipsum esse*). Since God is the source of God's existence, there is within God the full perfection of being.

The *actus purus* tenet necessarily implies that there is no change in God.[7] God is sheerly actual; there is no potential in God. Any changing thing has potential. It follows that God cannot change. It also follows that the unchanging God cannot have a 'real relation' with the transient world. To be open to the world of becoming involves introducing change into one's existence. God relates to the world through a 'mixed relation'.[8] The relation is real in one term (our relationship to God), but only logical in the other (God's relationship to us). The real term in the relationship is affected or changed, but the same is not true of the other term.

Depoortere sums it up well: 'For Thomas, it is more perfect not to move than to move, and it is more perfect not to have a relationship than it is to have one.'[9] But how can God express love if there is no real relation with God's creatures? God wills our good and acts for our good. But such an action affects only the beneficiary. God is unchanged. Divine love is expressed through the 'intelligent appetite', not through the 'sensitive appetite'. Indeed, there is no 'sensitive appetite' in God. The senses involve passion, and passion involves change. There is a movement from one emotional state to another. 'Loving, enjoying and delighting are emotions when they signify activities of the sensitive appetite; not so, however, when they signify activities of the intelligent appetite. It is in this last sense that they are attributed to God.'[10] God loves without passion.

In developing his argument that God does not suffer, the Oxford theologian Thomas Weinandy builds on these insights of Aquinas and includes them in a trinitarian framework.[11] The triune God loves us and acts fully and completely for our good, but does not feel, cannot feel, our pain.

Weinandy begins with the insight, shared by both Augustine and Aquinas, that what distinguishes the persons of the Trinity is their relationships (something we have also noted: see Chapters 1, 6 and 7). That is, they subsist as distinct persons in and through their relationships to one another. What defines the nature of these relationships is the actions of 'origination' and 'spiration'. The Father is constituted as Father in and through the eternal acts of begetting the Son and 'breathing forth' the Holy Spirit. The Son subsists eternally as the Son through being begotten by the Father and conformed by the Spirit to be the Son of the Father. Finally, nothing constitutes the Holy Spirit as Holy Spirit other than his (or her) proceeding from the Father and the Son and so shaping the Father–Son relationship in the Godhead. Thus, it is relationality that defines the Trinity. Each person is defined as who he (or she) singularly is, and so subsists as who he is, through the relationship he shares with the other two.

Now, if one takes on board Aquinas's doctrine that God is sheer actuality and therefore immune from change, the conclusion one reaches, argues Weinandy, is that Father, Son and Holy Spirit are subsistent relations fully in act and therefore immutable and impassible. He is aware that contemporary theologians frequently argue that such a view of God makes God look more like a stone than the dynamic, active, personal God of the Bible. Thus, he is quick to make the point that immutability in the Trinity does not imply inertness:

> [The persons of the Trinity] are immutable not because they are static or inert in their relationships, but precisely for the opposite reason. Because they are subsistent relations fully in act, because the terms 'Father', 'Son', and 'Holy Spirit' designate pure acts … they do not have any relational potential which would need to be actualized in order to make them more relational – more who they are. As subsistent relations fully in act, the persons of the Trinity are utterly and completely dynamic and active in their integral and comprehensive self-giving to one another, and could not possibly become any more dynamic or active in their self-giving since they are constituted, and so subsist, as who they are only in their complete and utter self-giving to one another.[12]

For Weinandy, then, Aquinas's view that God is immutable should not be taken to imply inertness. God is unchangeable not because God is static or inert like a stone, but for precisely the opposite reason. God is so active, so dynamic, that no change could make God more active. This dynamism is expressed in the life of the Trinity through relationship. The crux of Weinandy's argument is that God is *actus purus* and therefore has no potential to become more relational.

This absolutely dynamic relational life of the Trinity is extended to the world. God is at work in the world drawing human persons into this rich inner life. '[The] lack of any self-constituting relational potential, since they are subsistent relations fully in act, gives to the persons of the Trinity absolute positive relational potential, that is, they have the singular ability to establish relationships with others other than themselves whereby the persons of the Trinity can relate others to themselves as they are in themselves as a trinity of persons.'[13] Thus, according to this view the relationship offered to us by the Trinity is of the most intimate and dynamic kind possible.

Having developed his picture of the rich relational life of the Trinity, Weinandy goes on to construct his argument that there is no suffering in the Godhead. He works with the traditional theological view that evil, founded as it is upon the reality of sin, is a privation or absence of good. Consider, for example, the fact that sight is good, but blindness is the privation of the good of sight. Sex is good when accompanied by a loving intimacy, but the sexual act in the absence of love and intimacy degrades into lust. The absence of some good is the cause of evil. Sin, as the source of evil, deprives human beings of the goods God intends for us. It should now be clear why Weinandy contends that God cannot suffer. If there were suffering in the Godhead the triune persons would be blighted with a privation of the good:

> If the persons of the Trinity were infected with suffering, it would mean that they were deprived of some good, and so enmeshed in sin and evil. Thus they would no longer be subsistent relations fully in act possessing fully actualized love and goodness, but would now be in potency to obtaining or re-obtaining the good they did not possess. However, this

loss would render them impotent to create, and thus to relate to creatures themselves in the fullness of their love and goodness in an immediate, dynamic, intimate, and unbreakable manner.[14]

Weinandy is building the argument that *a God who does not suffer is actually more loving and more compassionate than a God who does*. Of course, the obvious objection is that it is difficult to see how we can talk meaningfully about love and compassion in one for whom suffering is never a possibility. To love someone is to risk the pain of misunderstanding and rejection. To love someone is to feel her pain with her. Weinandy attempts to counter this argument by building an analogy between human and divine love. For humans, love is a willingness to give of oneself for the good of another. Sometimes acting for the good of another, it is true, will also involve suffering. But suffering is not itself a constitutive element of love, argues Weinandy. Extending these observations to God's love, he believes that it is possible to see why the inability of God to suffer does not imply divine indifference. 'Since suffering is not constitutive of love, we can also perceive why the absence of suffering in God does not necessarily imply the absence of love and thus divine indifference. Actually, since God does not suffer, his love becomes absolutely free in its expression and supremely pure in its purpose.'[15]

While I was prepared to travel with Weinandy to the point where he argues for the fully actual and dynamic love in the life of the Trinity, I now find myself wanting to part company. I find it impossible to conceive of love and compassion expressed without an entry into the pain and grief of another. When we love another we are open to the experiences they bring. As Charles Hartshorne puts it: 'To love is to rejoice with the joys and sorrow with the sorrows of others. Thus it is to be influenced by those who are loved.'[16] To be fully available to others in love we must be receptive to their experiences of joy and pain. Gabriel Marcel says that to be truly available to others involves a certain in-cohesion.[17] We must be open enough to let the thoughts and feelings of others get into us. He uses the image of porousness. The one who is fully available has openings through which both the joy and the distress of others may enter.

Surely God, in God's love for us, must be able to sorrow with those who are sorrowing. I want to argue for an empathic God, a God who draws near to us in our distress and feels our hurt with us. Love and suffering are bound up together. Hartshorne puts it well: 'The chief novelty of the New Testament is that divine love … is carried to the point of participation in creaturely suffering, symbolized by the Cross taken together with the doctrine of the Incarnation.'[18]

Though Weinandy cannot accept this view that God's love is expressed through a participation in our suffering, he still wants to contend for a fullness of love in the Trinity. There is no self-actualizing potential in the persons in the Trinity and therefore it is impossible for them to be more loving. The divine persons never need to actualize some aspect of their love to become more loving. God can therefore be fully responsive to every situation that might occur.[19] God will sometimes be called upon to express love through goodness, affection, joy, kindness, courage and power. On other occasions – those marked by sin and rebellion – God will manifest the divine love through compassion, mercy, patience and forgiveness. All these facets of God's love are fully actualized and ready and available to be communicated to us. So

God is perfectly compassionate not because God suffers with us, but because we are fully embraced in our suffering by the divine love. God might not be able to grieve and sorrow with us,[20] but the divine love is most fully expressed through actions aimed at dispelling evil and restoring the good.[21]

I want to suggest, however, that this image of a God who does what is good for us without also participating in our suffering is not an especially attractive one. Such a God is available to us through good works but not through a personal, participatory engagement with our experience. This is a counterfeit form of availability. Marcel calls it 'constancy'. To make his point, he uses an example that we can all relate to. I want to call myself 'faithful friend' because I have fulfilled all my obligations vis-à-vis the other, X, but in the end cannot really do so because I act without making a personal connection. I may think that I have done all that is required of me. I have done all in my power to do what is good for X, but the real question is, How does it feel for X?

> Assuming that X learns in some way or other that I have behaved towards him in a *conscientious* way, it is likely that he will release me from this obligation at least in his conscience; there is then the possibility that he will say to me with an intonation that can have infinite variations: 'Don't think you are obligated to me ...' To be sure, he knows that my conduct has been irreproachable; however, or rather because of this very thing, something has been shattered within him; we can even say that in his view a certain value has been lost and that what remains is only straw – and it is here that we see the problem of fidelity dawn, strictly speaking.[22]

A 'constant God' is one who acts fully for our good but who does not at the same time participate in our sorrow and distress. While we appreciate the good this God does, 'a certain value has been lost and ... what remains is only straw'.

Frances Young is a British theologian who wrestles with the question of divine passibility in the context of the pain that she has lived with as a result of the profound mental disability of her son, Arthur. Young seems to concur with the sentiments I have just expressed. For her, 'an uninvolved "do-gooder" will not do'.[23] She points to the Old Testament where we encounter a God who is distressed by the waywardness of God's people and who lovingly yearns for their return. She thinks, as I do, that a personal God must be intimately involved, and therefore must truly suffer in response to human suffering. The focal point of God's suffering with us and for us is found in the cross. 'For many sufferers the only answer is the Cross – the fact of God suffering, God entering into all the travail and pain, taking responsibility for it, overcoming it.'[24]

Despite reaching the point of embracing a suffering God, there are still some niggling worries for Young. She wonders if God's changelessness and impassibility remain important theological ideas. 'For how can a vulnerable God still be God, a God to worship and depend upon? If you are tempted to sigh "Poor old God", what kind of a God are you left with?'[25] To deal with her discomfort Young develops a notion of a God who is *both passionate and passionless at the same time*. She draws an analogy with human emotions. On the one hand, we value the capacity to feel deeply with another. This indicates that a person is truly human. But on the other hand, we value peace, serenity and calm in a person. We all know how the storms of passion play havoc with us. To be able to bring powerful emotions under control and to think and act calmly and peacefully is accorded a high value. Extending this thinking to the reality of God, God is the one who is involved in our suffering but who is at the same time an ocean of peace and serenity. A personal experience of Young's helped shape this view of God:

> Early in 1988, a couple close to me had a tragic experience in relation to the birth of a child – their daughter was still-born. To say the least I felt for them. But after a while I realised that my distress was not just for them. I was re-living my own pain, my own struggle to understand how things could go wrong, my own anguish and protest at the suffering of the world. I was too involved, and it was only when the self-involvement was purged that I could begin to be of use to those who were suffering.[26]

This experience led Young to reclaim the traditional insight that God is 'beyond suffering' in the sense that God is not emotionally involved. Rather, God 'is the ocean of love that can absorb all the suffering of the world and purge it without being polluted or changed by it'.[27]

Clearly, this reappropriation of the traditional view of God is grounded in an important pastoral reality. If we allow ourselves to be overwhelmed by the pain we are encountering we are unable to offer effective pastoral care. The movement of our thoughts and feelings undergoes a reversal. When we are calm we are able to reach out to the other in her distress; but when we lose control of our emotions we retreat inwards. Our attention shifts from the person we are offering care to; we experience an inward turn to our own fears and concerns. Nevertheless, I contend that it is important to recognize that there are stages in between being completely uninvolved, on the one hand, and being totally overwhelmed, on the other. It is possible to be emotionally connected to a person and her suffering while still maintaining the calm and self-control that are needed for effective action. This is, in fact, the picture we get of God through the scriptures. In the Hebrew Scriptures, we read of how God is grieved by the infidelity of the people. The pain of unrequited love comes home to God, and yet God is still very much in command of the situation. When it is required, God disciplines the people. Then, when the people cry out in their distress, God hears and acts to deliver them.

The focal point of the story of the Christian Scriptures is God's saving action through the cross. Though the Father is deeply grieved by the giving up of his Son, he is able to act to overcome Golgotha. In the resurrection we see God's 'correction' or 'un-doing' (Depoortere) of suffering and death. God feels our pain but is not paralysed by it. Profound empathy and decisive action are not mutually exclusive realities.

Young does not see it this way, though. The only solution for her is a paradoxical assertion that God is both passionless and passionate. God is the ocean of calm in which all the pain and anguish of the world is absorbed, but at the same time God is personally involved in suffering through the cross of Christ. God in Christ 'unsufferingly suffered'.[28] How is it possible to hold these opposites together in the one God? Young turns to the thinking of the Greek Fathers and states that God is impassible in God's essence, but 'possible' in Christ.

While I agree that the focal point for the suffering of God is the cross, I cannot support this dividing up of the experience in the Godhead. Moltmann seems much closer to the truth in his portrayal of the passion and death of Christ as a trinitarian event. The cross involves both the Father and the Son in the experience of suffering. I will have more to say about this below. But first we need to acknowledge that the 'tears of God' (Harrington) are not to be found only on Golgotha. Fiddes is right when he says that we must develop a portrait of 'a God who suffers universally and yet is still present uniquely in the suffering of Christ'.[29] In the Hebrew Scriptures we also find a story of God's suffering love. The cross is an intensification and a deepening of God's perpetual suffering.[30]

The Story of God's Suffering

Throughout the Bible we find a picture of a suffering God. In a beautifully written work, Wilfrid Harrington points us to the central narratives in relation to this presentation of God.[31] He observes that the first outlines of the presentation, those found in the Old Testament, reveal a grieving and a lamenting God.

The story of God's grief begins with God's free choice to create a partner for Godself. In freedom and in love there is, as Barth puts it, an 'overflow' of the divine essence.[32] God does not will to be God alone, to be God for Godself, but God with us and for us. God chooses dialogue, and all dialogue involves risk. The risk is that one's overtures of love will be spurned. In the Hebrew Scriptures, we encounter a story of God reaching out to humankind, only to suffer the grief of rejection. The Flood story tells of a God who sorrows deeply over the human response to the offer of partnership. 'Yahweh regretted having made human beings on the earth and was grieved at heart. And Yahweh said, "I shall rid the surface of the earth of the human beings whom I created … for I regret having made them"' (Gen. 6:6–7). Harrington suggests that it is not because God has made a horrible mistake in choosing dialogue that God feels sorrow and grief.[33] Rather, the pain in the divine heart is the result of the wholesale rejection of God's love and grace. God *has* to respond to this situation. At first, the wrath of God rages and the earth is flooded. But then comes the abrogation of the decision to blot out humankind: 'Never again will I curse the earth because of human beings, because their heart contrives evil from their infancy. Never again will I strike down every living thing as I have done' (Gen. 8:21). God has decided to live with humankind's tendency to evil.

The persistent rebellious streak in human beings is a dominant theme in the story of Yahweh's covenantal relationship with Israel. God chose Israel to be God's own and lavishes blessings upon the people. But time and time again they wander from the straight path that Yahweh has set before them. 'I thought: You will call me Father and will never cease to follow me. But like a woman betraying her lover, House of Israel, you have betrayed me …' (Jer. 3:19b–20). Israel is God's own and God is faithful in God's love for her. When God is faced with infidelity, the heart of God is grieved: 'My people are bent on disregarding me; if they are summoned to come up, not one of them makes a move … My heart within me is overwhelmed, fever grips my inmost being' (Hos. 11:7, 8c).

The story of the suffering of God manifested in God's covenantal relationship with Israel reaches a climax in the passion and death of Jesus. The grieving God, the lamenting God, becomes the crucified God. Traditional theology was happy to attach the suffering of the cross to the human nature of Jesus, but kept his divine nature immune from it. Jürgen Moltmann, however, has shown that the passion of Jesus is really a divine passion.[34] This divine passion is an event in the trinitarian life of God. The Father suffers the grief of giving over the Son, and the Son suffers the pain of 'godforsakenness'. It is here that we find the special element in the passion of Christ. Many other righteous and innocent people have suffered terribly. What sets Jesus's suffering apart is the ineffable pain of abandonment by the Father.[35]

Dorothee Soelle claims that this is, in fact, a misunderstanding of the significance of the passion.[36] 'This way of stating the issue, that in a world of immeasurable suffering wants to isolate Jesus' suffering and make it something that outweighs the rest in order to be able to understand it as unique, is rather macabre. It is not in Jesus' best interest to have suffered "the most".'[37] For Soelle, the real truth in the symbol of the cross is not its uniqueness but rather 'its repeatability'. Those who are suffering, she argues, are able to draw comfort from Christ's passion because they feel connected to it. They can appropriate the cross only if they feel that there is a link between their experience and that of Jesus. Repeatabilty, then, is the condition of the possibility of the cross acting as a source of consolation.

Here I would make two comments. The first relates to Soelle's suggestion that there is a 'macabre' element in the contention that Jesus's suffering outweighs all the rest. I do not believe that Moltmann's aim is to show that of all those righteous and innocent ones who have suffered in human history Jesus has suffered the most. Rather, he wants to point out that the suffering of other godly persons cannot be 'on the same level' as that of Jesus.[38] This is so because of the special element of abandonment by the One whom he calls 'Abba'. It is the question of the uniqueness in the suffering of Jesus that Moltmann is addressing. The language of 'levels' of suffering refers to a qualitative rather than a quantitative distinction.

I would also make the point that the fact that the passion and death of Jesus has a unique element to it does not automatically mean that suffering persons will find it very difficult to connect with. For along with the special element in that experience there is also a common element. As well as the unique pain associated with the rupture in the relationships in the Godhead, there is the pain that is shared by many. In my experience, those who feel tortured through either deep mental or physical suffering, or through both, can quite readily identify with the agony Jesus suffered. Awareness of the special nature of Jesus's suffering will not prevent a suffering person from connecting with his experience.

This godforsakenness that constitutes the special aspect of Jesus's suffering first appears in the garden at Gethsemane. The 'cup' that Jesus prays may pass is the suffering associated with separation from the Father. But the Father does not offer to take the cup from Jesus. 'This *unanswered prayer* is the beginning of Jesus's real passion – his agony at his forsakenness by the Father.'[39]

At the end of Christ's passion there is another prayer, namely the despairing cry to God with which Christ dies: 'My God, why have you forsaken me?' (Mark 15:34). Here is 'an expression of the most profound rejection by the God whom he called "Abba"'.[40] But it is not only the Son who is pained in and through the event of the cross. The son may lose his sonship, but the father also loses his fatherhood. The Son suffers the pain of abandonment, and the Father the grief of giving up his beloved. Here we see 'the breakdown of the relationship that constitutes the very life of the Trinity'.[41]

On Golgotha the Father and the Son are separated, and yet at the same time they also remain bound together. They are bound together through their common commitment to an act of surrendering love. This surrender through the Father in which there is an offering of the Son takes place through the Spirit. 'The Holy Spirit is ... the link in the separation. He is the link joining the bond between the Father and the Son, with their separation.'[42] The cross constitutes a trinitarian experience of suffering.

Summary

The reason why I have been so intent on demonstrating the reality of God's suffering is that I have been aiming at a 'theodicy of consolation' (Fiddes). Those whom we encounter in our pastoral work are comforted by the empathy and support that we offer. But they also look for consolation from God. To know that God is not an 'ivory tower' deity but rather one who participates in suffering is a great comfort.

Throughout the Hebrew Scriptures we read of a grieving, sorrowing God. God chose dialogue and so opened Godself to the arrows of rejection. The suffering of God reaches a climax in the passion and death of Jesus. The grieving and lamenting God becomes a crucified God. Divine love is so deep that God was prepared to endure the ineffable hurt of a rupture in the inner life of the Godhead.

Ours is an empathic God. The Great Companion knows what it is to suffer deeply. God understands our pain and draws very near to us in love and grace.

Notes

1   A.N. Whitehead, *Process and Reality* (New York: Harper & Row, 1960), p. 532.
2   J. Robbins, 'Theological Table-Talk: A Pastoral Approach to Evil', *Theology Today* 44 (1988), pp. 488–95 (p. 491).
3   See T. Weinandy, *Does God Suffer?* (Edinburgh: T. & T. Clark, 2000).
4   Aquinas, *Summa Theologiae*, Ia.3.1. I have used the edition trans. by T. Gilby (London: Eyre & Spottiswoode, 1964–5).
5   *Summa*, Ia.3.1.
6   *Summa*, Ia.4.2.
7   *Summa*, Ia.9.1.
8   See Weinandy, *Does God Suffer?*, p. 130.
9   K. Depoortere, *A Different God* (Louvain: Peeters Press, and Grand Rapids, Mich.: Eerdmans, 1995), p. 91.
10   Aquinas, *Summa*, Ia.20.1.
11   See Weinandy, *Does God Suffer?*, pp. 115–71.
12   Ibid., p. 119.
13   Ibid., p. 128.
14   Ibid., p. 158.

15 Ibid., p. 160.
16 C. Hartshorne, *A Natural Theology for Our Time* (Lasalle, Ill.: Open Court, 1967), p. 75.
17 See G. Marcel, *Creative Fidelity*, trans. R. Rosthal (New York: Noonday Press, 1964), pp. 87–8.
18 Ibid., pp. 104–5.
19 See Weinandy, *Does God Suffer?*, p. 162.
20 We should note that while Weinandy denies that God experiences sorrow as a negative passible state, he does suggest that it can reside in God as a positive facet of God's perfectly actualized love. See *Does God Suffer?*, p. 165.
21 See ibid., pp. 167–8.
22 Ibid., p. 155.
23 F. Young, *Face to Face* (Edinburgh: T. & T. Clark, 1990), p. 238.
24 Ibid., p. 238.
25 Ibid., p. 237.
26 Ibid., pp. 238–9.
27 Ibid., p. 239.
28 Ibid., p. 247.
29 P. Fiddes, *The Creative Suffering of God* (Oxford: Clarendon Press, 1988), p. 2.
30 Cf. ibid., p. 8.
31 See W. Harrington, *The Tears of God* (Collegeville, Minn.: Liturgical Press, 1992).
32 K. Barth, *Church Dogmatics*, II/1 (Edinburgh: T. & T. Clark, 1957), p. 273.
33 See Harrington, *The Tears of God*, p. 20.
34 See J. Moltmann, *The Crucified God* (London: SCM Press, 1974), p. 201ff; idem, *The Trinity and the Kingdom of God* (London: SCM Press, 1981), p. 75ff.
35 See Moltmann, *The Crucified God*, p. 53ff; idem, *Trinity and the Kingdom*, p. 75.
36 See D. Soelle, *Suffering* (Philadelphia: Fortress Press, 1975), pp. 81–2.
37 Ibid., p. 81.
38 See Moltmann, *The Crucified God*, p. 56.
39 Moltmann, *The Trinity and the Kingdom*, p. 76.
40 Ibid., p. 78.
41 Ibid., p. 80.
42 Ibid., p. 82.

Bibliography

Anderson, E.B., 'A Constructive Task in Religious Education: Making Christian Selves', *Religious Education* 93:2 (1998), 173–88.

Aquinas, T., *Summa Theologiae*, trans. T. Gilby (London: Eyre & Spottiswoode, 1964, 1965).

Augustine, *The Trinity*, trans. S. McKenna (Boston: St Paul Editions, 1965).

Avis, P., *Eros and the Sacred* (London: SPCK, 1989).

Balthasar, H.U. von, *The Glory of the Lord*, vol. 7: *Theology: The New Covenant* (Edinburgh: T. & T. Clark, 1989).

Barrett-Lennard, G., *Carl Rogers' Helping System: Journey and Substance* (London: SAGE Publications, 1998).

Barth, K., *Church Dogmatics*, I.1.8.3: *Vestigium Trinitatis* (Edinburgh, T. & T. Clark, 1936).

—— *Church Dogmatics*, II/1 (Edinburgh: T. & T. Clark, 1957).

Basil the Great, *The Nine Homilies of the Hexaemeron and the Letters*, in *A Select Library of Nicene and Post-Nicene Fathers*, vol. 8 (Grand Rapids, Mich.: Eerdmans, 1978).

—— *De Spiritu Sancto*, trans. B. Jackson, in *A Select Library of Nicene and Post-Nicene Fathers*, vol. 8 (Grand Rapids, Mich.: Eerdmans, 1978).

Berecz, J., 'All that Glitters Is Not Gold: Bad Forgiveness in Counseling and Preaching', *Pastoral Psychology* 49:4 (2001), 253–75.

Boff, L., *Holy Trinity, Perfect Community* (New York: Orbis Books, 2000).

Browning, D., *The Moral Context of Care* (Philadelphia: Westminster Press, 1976).

—— *Religious Ethics and Pastoral Care* (Minneapolis: Fortress Press, 1983).

Buber, M., *I and You*, trans. W. Kaufmann (Edinburgh: T. & T. Clark, 1970) [first published 1919].

Byrne, B., *The Hospitality of God: A Reading of Luke's Gospel* (Sydney: St Pauls, 2000).

Campbell, A., *Moderated Love: A Theology of Professional Care* (London: SPCK, 1984).

—— *Rediscovering Pastoral Care*, 2nd edn (London: Darton, Longman and Todd, 1986).

Capps, D., *Life Cycle Theory and Pastoral Care* (Philadelphia: Fortress Press, 1983).

—— *Reframing: A New Method in Pastoral Care* (Minneapolis: Fortress Press, 1990).

—— *The Depleted Self: Sin in a Narcissistic Age* (Minneapolis: Fortress Press, 1993).

Cave, T., 'Fictional Identities', in H. Harris (ed.), *Identity* (Oxford: Clarendon Press, 1995).

Cissna, K. and Anderson, R., 'The Contributions of Carl R. Rogers to a Philosophical Praxis of Dialogue', *Western Journal of Speech Communication* 54 (spring 1990), 125–47.

Cunningham, D., *These Three Are One: The Practice of Trinitarian Theology* (Oxford: Blackwell, 1998).

—— 'Participation as a Trinitarian Virtue', *Toronto Journal of Theology* 14:1 (1998), 7–25.

Depoortere, K., *A Different God* (Louvain: Peeters Press, and Grand Rapids, Mich.: Eerdmans, 1995).

Drewery, W. and Winslade, J., 'The Theoretical Story of Narrative Therapy', in G. Monk et al (eds), *Narrative Therapy in Practice* (San Francisco: Jossey-Bass, 1997).

Drilling, T., *Trinity and Ministry* (Minneapolis: Fortress Press, 1991).

Duan, C. and Hill, C., 'The Current State of Empathy Research', *Journal of Counseling Psychology* 43:3 (1996), 261–74.

Egan, G., *The Skilled Helper*, 4th edn (Pacific Grove, Calif.: Brooks/Cole, 1990).

Erikson, E.H., *Identity and the Life Cycle* (New York: International Universities Press, 1959).

Fiddes, P., *The Creative Suffering of God* (Oxford: Clarendon Press, 1988).

—— *Participating in God: A Pastoral Doctrine of the Trinity* (London: Darton, Longman and Todd, 2000).

Fox, P., *God as Communion* (Collegeville, Minn.: Liturgical Press, 2001).

Freedman, J. and Combs, G., *Narrative Therapy* (New York: W.W. Norton, 1996).

Friedman, M., 'Buber's Philosophy as the Basis for Dialogical Psychotherapy and Contextual Therapy', *Journal of Humanistic Psychology* 38 (1998), 25–40.

Gaillardetz, R., 'In Service of Communion', *Worship* 67 (1993), 418–33.

Gilligan, C., *In a Different Voice: Psychological Theory and Women's Development* (Cambridge, Mass.: Harvard University Press, 1982).

Goodliff, P., *Care in a Confused Climate* (London: Darton, Longman and Todd, 1998).

Graham, L., *Care of Persons, Care of Worlds* (Nashville, Tenn.: Abingdon Press, 1992).

Gregory of Nyssa, *Against Eunomius*, Book I, in *A Select Library of Nicene and Post-Nicene Fathers*, vol. 5 (Grand Rapids, Mich.: Eerdmans, 1988).

Grenz, S., *Rediscovering the Triune God: The Trinity in Contemporary Theology* (Minneapolis: Fortress Press, 2004).

Gunton, C., *The Promise of Trinitarian Theology* (Edinburgh: T. & T. Clark, 1991).

—— 'The God of Jesus Christ', *Theology Today* 54:3 (1997), 325–34.

—— *Intellect and Action* (Edinburgh: T. & T. Clark, 2000).

Harrington, W., *The Tears of God* (Collegeville, Minn.: Liturgical Press, 1992).

Harter, S., *The Construction of the Self: A Developmental Perspective* (New York: Guilford Press, 1999).

Hartshorne, C., *A Natural Theology for Our Time* (Lasalle, Ill.: Open Court, 1967).

Hitlin, S., 'Values as the Core of Personal Identity: Drawing Links between Two Theories of Self', *Social Psychology Quarterly* 66:2 (2003), 118–37.

Hobson, R., *Forms of Feeling* (London: Tavistock Publications, 1985).

Hoffman, J., *Ethical Confrontation in Counseling* (University of Chicago Press, 1979).

Hycner, R., *Between Person and Person* (Highland, NY: Gestalt Journal, 1991).

Jacques, F., *Difference and Subjectivity*, trans. A. Rothwell (New Haven, Conn.: Yale University Press, 1991).

Johnson, L.T., 'Making Connections: The Material Expression of Fellowship in the New Testament', *Interpretation* 58:2 (2004), 158–71.

Karen, R., 'Shame', *Atlantic Monthly* (Feb. 1992), 40–70.

Kelly, A., *The Trinity of Love* (Wilmington, Del.: Michael Glazier, 1989).

Kohut, H., *The Analysis of the Self* (New York: International Universities Press, 1971).

—— *The Restoration of the Self* (New York: International Universities Press, 1977).

—— *The Search for the Self*, ed. P. Ornstein (New York: International Universities Press, 1978).

—— *How Does Analysis Cure?* (Chicago: University of Chicago Press, 1984).

LaCugna, C.M., *God for Us: The Trinity and Christian Life* (HarperSanFrancisco, 1991).

Lester, A., *Pastoral Care with Children in Crisis* (Philadelphia: Westminster Press, 1985).

Leupp, R., *Knowing the Name of God: A Trinitarian Tapestry of Grace, Faith and Community* (Downers Grove, Ill.: InterVarsity Press, 1995).

Lounibos, J.B., 'Self-Emptying in Christian and Buddhist Spirituality', *Journal of Pastoral Counseling* 35 (2000), 49–66.

McCarthy, M., 'Empathy: A Bridge Between', *Journal of Pastoral Care* 46:2 (1992), 119–28.

McDougall, J.A., 'The Return of Trinitarian Praxis? Moltmann on the Trinity and the Christian Life', *Journal of Religion* 83:2 (2003), 177–203.

McEnhill, P. and Newlands, G., *Fifty Key Christian Thinkers* (London: Routledge, 2004).

McKenzie, W. and Monk, G., 'Learning and Teaching Narrative Ideas', in G. Monk et al (eds), *Narrative Therapy in Practice* (San Francisco: Jossey-Bass, 1997).

Macmurray, J., *Persons in Relation* (London: Faber and Faber, 1961).

Marcel, G.,*Creative Fidelity*, trans. R. Rosthal (New York: Noonday Press, 1964).

Margulies, A., *The Empathic Imagination* (New York: W.W. Norton, 1989).

May, R., *Love and Will* (London: Souvenir Press, 1970).

Merton, T., *Seeds of Contemplation* (London: Burns and Oates, 1949, 1957).

Mitchell, D.W., 'Re-Creating Christian Community: A Response to Rita M. Gross', *Buddhist-Christian Studies* 23 (2003), 21–32.

Moltmann, J., *The Crucified God* (London: SCM Press, 1974).

—— *The Trinity and the Kingdom of God* (London: SCM Press, 1981).

—— *History and the Triune God* (New York: Crossroad, 1992).

—— *The Spirit of Life: A Universal Affirmation* (Philadelphia: Fortress Press, 1992).

—— 'Perichoresis: An Old Magic Word for a New Trinitarian Theology', in M.D. Meeks (ed.), *Trinity, Power and Community* (Nashville, Tenn.: Kingswood Books, 2000).

Monk, G., 'How Narrative Therapy Works', in G. Monk et al (eds), *Narrative Therapy in Practice* (San Francisco: Jossey-Bass, 1997).

Morgan, A., *What is Narrative Therapy?* (Adelaide: Dulwich Centre Publications, 2000).

Morrison, A.P., 'Shame, Ideal Self, and Narcissism', in A.P. Morrison (ed.), *Essential Papers on Narcissism* (New York University Press, 1986).

Nin, A., *The Journals of Anaïs Nin, 1931–1934*, ed. G. Stuhlmann (London: Peter Owen, 1966).

Nouwen, H., *The Wounded Healer* (Garden City, NY: Doubleday, 1972).

—— *Reaching Out* (New York: Doubleday, 1975).

Nygren, A., *Agape and Eros*, parts I and II (London: SPCK, 1932, 1939).

Olthuis, J., 'Being-with: Toward a Relational Psychotherapy', *Journal of Psychology and Christianity* 13 (1994), 217–31.

—— 'Dancing Together in the Wild Spaces of Love: Postmodernism, Psychotherapy, and the Spirit of God', *Journal of Psychology and Christianity* 18 (1999), 140–52.

Outka, G., *Agape: An Ethical Analysis* (New Haven, Conn.: Yale University Press, 1972).

Pattison, S., *Pastoral Care and Liberation Theology* (Cambridge University Press, 1994).

Peck, M.S., *The Road Less Travelled* (London: Arrow Books, 1990) [first published 1978].

Pembroke, N., *The Art of Listening: Dialogue, Shame, and Pastoral Care* (Grand Rapids, Mich.: Eerdmans, 2002).

Peters, T., *God as Trinity: Relationality and Temporality in Divine Life* (Louisville, Ky.: Westminster/John Knox Press, 1993).

Pohl, C., *Making Room: Recovering Hospitality as a Christian Tradition* (Grand Rapids, Mich.: Eerdmans, 1999).

Poling, J., *Deliver Us from Evil: Resisting Racial and Gender Oppression* (Minneapolis: Fortress Press, 1996).

Post, S., 'The Inadequacy of Selflessness', *Journal of the American Academy of Religion* 56:2 (1989), 213–23.

Rahner, K., *The Trinity*, trans. J. Donceel (London: Burns and Oates, 1970).

Robbins, J., 'Theological Table-Talk: A Pastoral Approach to Evil', *Theology Today* 44 (1988), 488–95.

Rogers, C., 'A Theory of Therapy, Personality, and Interpersonal Relationships as Developed in the Client-Centered Framework', in S. Koch (ed.), *Psychology: A Study of a Science*, vol. 3 (New York: McGraw-Hill, 1959).

—— *A Way of Being* (Boston: Houghton Mifflin, 1980).

—— *The Carl Rogers Reader*, ed. H. Kirschenbaum and V. Land Henderson (London: Constable, 1990).

Rowan, J., *Subpersonalities: The People Inside Us* (London: Routledge, 1990).

Russell, L., 'Practicing Hospitality in a Time of Backlash', *Theology Today* 52 (1996), 477–85.

Savage, J., *Listening and Caring Skills in Ministry* (Nashville, Tenn.: Abingdon Press, 1996).

Scirghi, T.J., 'The Trinity: A Model for Belonging in Contemporary Society', *Ecumenical Review* 54:3 (2002), 333–42.

Soelle, D., *Suffering* (Philadelphia: Fortress Press, 1975).

Thompson, J. *Modern Trinitarian Perspectives* (Oxford University Press, 1994).

Thorne, B., *Person-Centred Counselling: Therapeutic and Spiritual Dimensions* (London: Whurr, 1991).

Tillich, P., *Love, Power and Justice* (Oxford University Press, 1954).

—— *Systematic Theology*, vol. 2 (University of Chicago Press, 1957).

Vacek, E., *Love, Human and Divine: The Heart of Christian Ethics* (Washington, DC: Georgetown University Press, 1994).

Wadell, P., *Becoming Friends: Worship, Justice, and the Practice of Christian Friendship* (Grand Rapids, Mich.: Brazos Press, 2002).

Waterman, A., 'Identity Formation: Discovery or Creation?', *Journal of Early Adolescence* 4:4 (1984), 329–41.

Weil, S., *Waiting on God* (London: Routledge and Kegan Paul, 1951).

Weinandy, T., *Does God Suffer?* (Edinburgh: T. & T. Clark, 2000).

White, C., *Christian Friendship in the Fourth Century* (Cambridge University Press, 1992).

White, M. and Epston, D., *Narrative Means to Therapeutic Ends* (Adelaide: Dulwich Centre Publications, 1990).

Whitehead, A.N., *Process and Reality* (New York: Harper & Row, 1960).

Winslade, J. and Monk, G., *Narrative Counseling in Schools* (Thousand Oaks, Calif.: Sage Publications, 1999).

Wuthnow, R., 'Small Groups Forge New Notions of Community and the Sacred', *Christian Century* 110:35 (8 Dec. 1993), 1236–40.

Young, F., *Face to Face* (Edinburgh: T. & T. Clark, 1990).

Zizioulas, J., *Being as Communion* (Crestwood, NY: St Vladimir's Seminary Press, 1985).

—— 'On Being a Person: Towards an Ontology of Personhood', in C. Schwobel and C. Gunton (eds), *Persons, Divine and Human* (Edinburgh: T. & T. Clark, 1991).

Index

and love, three forms of 90–91
and passion of Christ 103–106
and *perichoresis* 2, 10, 43, 48, 51, 66, 72
and processions 13, 23, 90–91, 99
and self-communication 2, 10–12, 47
and *vestigia trinitatis* 7, 14, 62
true self 36–8

Vacek, E. 84–5

vestigia trinitatis 7, 14, 62

Weil, S. 47, 51, 53
Weinandy, T. 99–101
Whitehead, A.N. 97

Young, F. 102–103

Zizioulas, J. 69–71, 74